MODERN
FASCISM

EZRA POUND: poet, critic, and godfather of modernism. Pound was also a propagandist for Mussolini. Arrested for treason at the end of World War II, Pound was committed to a mental hospital until 1958. Upon his release, at the urging of America's literary and intellectual establishment, Pound returned to Italy. The photograph shows him upon his arrival on the liner Christoforo Colombo in Naples, Italy, in April 1958, at age 72, affirming his post-Holocaust National Socialism with the fascist salute. For further information, see especially pages 116–118 and *Ezra Pound* in the index.

CONCORDIA
SCHOLARSHIP
Today

MODERN
FASCISM

Liquidating the Judeo-Christian
Worldview

Gene Edward Veith, Jr.

CPH.
SAINT LOUIS

The author and the publisher gratefully acknowledge permission to reprint material from the following:

Mein Kampf by Adolf Hitler, tr. Ralph Manheim. Copyright 1943 and © renewed by Houghton Mifflin Company. Reprinted by permission Houghton Mifflin Company. All rights reserved.

Ezra Pound: The Cantos of Ezra Pound. Copyright 1934 by Ezra Pound. Reprinted by permission of New Direction Press.

Heidegger and Nazism by Victor Farias, tr. Paul Burell. Copyright 1989 by Temple University. Reprinted by permission of Temple University Press.

"The Barmen Declaration," published in *The Encyclopedia of American Religions: Religious Creeds*, First Edition, edited by J. Gordon Melton. Copyright © 1988 by Gale Research Inc. Reprinted by permission of the publisher.

"Fascist Ideology" by Zeev Sternhell, in Walter Laqueur, ed. *Fascism, A Reader's Guide: Analysis, Interpretations, and Bibliography.* Copyright © 1976 Walter Laqueur.

The Deconstruction of Literature: Criticism after Auschwitz by David N. Hirsch. Hanover, NH: Brown University Press, 1991. Reprinted by permission.

Copyright © 1993 Concordia Publishing House
3558 S. Jefferson Avenue, St. Louis, MO 63118-3968
Manufactured in the United States of America

Library of Congress Cataloging-in-Publication Data

Veith, Gene Edward, 1951–
      Modern fascism : liquidating the Judeo-Christian worldview / Gene Edward Veith, Jr.
        p.   cm. — (Concordia scholarship today)
      ISBN 0-570-04603-3
      1. Fascism. 2. Fascist ethics. 3. Intellectuals. 4. Immanence (Philosophy) 5. Transcendence (Philosophy) I. Title. II. Series.
JC481.V36   1993
320.5'33—dc20   92-41904

6   7   8   9   10   02   01   00

To the memory of my late colleague,
Professor William Houser

Contents

Foreword

Like all volumes in the Concordia Scholarship Today series, this book offers insights that relate to current concerns. The assumption is that an analysis and clarification of issues that beset us today, viewed against a broadened and deepened understanding of the Christian faith, will lead us to make considered and responsible applications and in so doing help us to "comprehend the love of God in Christ" (Eph. 3: 17–18).

In exploring the issues in this book, Christian responsibility and integrity are a primary concern. While the reader may differ with the author's analyses and/or interpretations, the following must be among our overriding common concerns: Biblical teachings related to the issue must be clearly defined without compromise. Biblical doctrine needs to be distinguished from the practice or application of doctrine. Information and alternative choices must be carefully considered and clearly understood.

Ideas have consequences. That truism is frightening, even for the most astute analysts and thinkers, in a day when a whirlpool of confusing ideological currents seems to engulf us. In recent years the alarm bell has been sounded in a spate of books and articles by perceptive and insightful authors, warning us to be watchful in every corner of life—*Illiberal Education* by Dinesh D'Souza; *Profscam* by Charles Sykes; *Under God: Religion and American Politics* by Gary Wills; *Defending the Declaration* by Gary Amos; *Agenda for Theology: After Modernity—What?* by Thomas C. Oden; "The Hands That Would Shape Our Souls" by Paul Wilkes (*Atlantic Monthly*, December 1990); *The Prodigal Press* by Marvin Olasky; and many more. All clearly show that analyzing trends in order to find a modus vivendi is becoming so challenging and intractable that it soon may elude us completely.

Earlier, Dr. Gene Edward Veith, Jr., offered a positive personal perspective for conscientious Christians in *Loving God with All Your*

Mind (Crossway, 1987). In *Reading Between the Lines* (Crossway, 1990) he offered substantive, practical, Christian guidelines for critical reading of literature. Here, in *Modern Fascism: Liquidating the Judeo-Christian Worldview,* he renders invaluable service by clearly singling out and defining fascism, a complex core of ideas that exalts the nation-state or race, disregards the individual and the individual's rights, employs thought control and strict regimentation, and disregards moral objectivity, sweeping everything and every one in its wake. The author shows how fascism is shaping society today, unwittingly as well as knowingly. He carefully clarifies fascism's relation to other ideas that likewise mold our thinking. Most important, he skillfully and convincingly combines historical narrative, cultural criticism, and theological analysis, offering much-needed guidance and hope for Americans, jostled and shaken by numerous ideological crosscurrents that threaten personal tranquillity and stability.

A reading of *Modern Fascism* shows that Dr. Veith has indirectly exposed the fallacy in the very common criticism that belief in theological dogma inhibits an open-minded search for knowledge and truth. He convincingly demonstrates that Christian theology provides a useful framework for acquiring and for integrating knowledge and in no way stifles the pursuit of truth. A sincere, conscientious effort to clarify biblical principles and apply them is far superior to relying on a framework of secular relativism in a society that prides itself on pluralism and individualism and yet in some respects is captive to fascist-type domination. In true Christian fashion, Dr. Veith exposes, explains, and counsels without dogmatically prescribing responses. In so doing, he achieves a difficult goal he has set for himself of clarifying the connection that often goes unnoticed between fascism and existentialism, theological liberalism, and the avant garde. This is a book that makes a difference.

The Publisher

Preface

Fascism is back. That is, it refuses to go away. Fifty years after World War II, it keeps intruding upon our attention in odd facts and disturbing news: Mussolini's 29-year-old granddaughter runs for parliament in Italy on a neofascist ticket. Former member of the American Nazi party David Duke runs for president of the United States. Despite media attention and some populist support, Duke meets ignominious defeat; but Allesandra Mussolini, along with 34 other members of the new fascist party, is elected.

Skinheads with their shaved heads and combat boots seem to be everywhere in Europe, staging soccer riots, beating up foreigners, painting swastika graffiti. In the United States, young skinheads are passing out racist literature on street corners and bolstering the membership of neo-Nazi cults such as the Aryan Nation.

The lunatic fringe, of course, is always with us, but we are also being confronted by signs of fascism as a larger social movement. Germany is having race riots again. The French are electing more and more neofascists to parliament. The implosion of communism was a great victory for democracy, but the vacuum has been filled by intense, violent ethnic nationalism and the revival of overt fascist movements that had been suppressed since World War II but are still very much alive. When Boris Yeltsin says that he is worried about a fascist coup in Russia, he has cause to worry, and so do we.

In the meantime, unsettling cultural trends are intensifying throughout the West: cynicism about democracy; a yearning for "charismatic leadership"; economic disaffection; moral skepticism, a cultural irrationalism that breaks out in acts of inexplicable violence.

Fascism is back in academia. A recent biography of the existentialist sage Martin Heidegger has uncovered his extensive involvement in the Nazi party. Those influenced by him—theorists, critics, and theologians—do not know quite what to do. Many are rushing

11

to his defense; many are taking a second look at the most influential philosopher of the 20th century.

Soon on the heels of the Heidegger scandal was the revelation that the major deconstructionist critic Paul De Man had written anti-Semitic articles for fascist newspapers. This news staggered the postmodern theorists with their leftist politics and their rejection of all authority. Many scholars simply cannot reconcile the intellectual sophistication of Heidegger and the progressive skepticism of De Man with the brutality of fascism. It turns out that many of these scholars, like the public as a whole, have a strange gap in their learning, a sort of collective amnesia: They have no clear idea of what fascism actually taught.

Thus far more disturbing than the personal failings of Heidegger and De Man is the ideology that is coalescing (partly from their influence) in today's intellectual establishment. Cultural determinism, the reduction of all social relationships to issues of sheer power; the idea that one's identity is centered in one's ethnicity or race; the rejection of the concept of the individual—such ideas have become academic commonplaces. The project in contemporary thought of dismantling Western civilization and critiquing "humanist" values (such as liberty, reason, and objective moral principles) is not new. All of these ideas are direct echoes of the fascist theorists of the 1930s.

The popular culture is the most fertile breeding ground for fascism. In the 1930s, avant-garde artists shocked the bourgeoisie with their aesthetic theories that glorified violence and the release of primitive emotions. Today, if you would like examples of early fascist aesthetics, simply go to the latest Hollywood blockbuster, turn on MTV, or go to a Heavy Metal concert. Here you will see realized the fascists' artistic ideals: pleasure from violence; the thrill of moral rebellion; the cult of the Aryan body. The grisly bloodletting of a slasher movie; the body-builder who takes the law into his own hands by machine-gunning his enemies; the masses of teenagers slam-dancing as Metallica sings, "Scream, as I'm killing you!"—such art is the quintessence of the fascist aesthetic.

Contemporary mass politics is very different from the democratic ideals of Madison and Jefferson. Instead of rational analysis of issues and reasoned debate, our political discourse turns on image manipulation through the mass media. The electronic media has created a genuine mass culture. Visual images take the place of language; emotionalism takes the place of logic. Politics is trivialized; citizens are manipulated, but they are molded into a common will. This was Goebbel's dream.

Moral issues are today almost impossible to discuss in objective terms. Euthanasia is back. People clamor for their right to die. One out of four pregnancies ends in abortion, amounting to millions and millions. In discussing such issues, it becomes evident that perhaps the majority of people today have no concept of an objective morality that transcends the individual and the culture. Morality is reduced to social utility or the assertion of the will. This was precisely the Nazi ethic.

Only five decades ago, the world was in the nightmare of war and Holocaust. We seem to have forgotten everything. Putting aside the images of goose-stepping villains from the movies, does anyone remember exactly what the fascists believed? Such forgetfulness is probably natural—after waking from a nightmare, the conscious mind erases its memory as soon as it can. But the nightmare of 50 years ago was no dream. It really happened, and we must be diligent lest it happen again.

We must know what fascism is so that we can recognize it when we see it. This will mean undoing certain misconceptions. Fascism is *not* conservatism. It is *not* the "right wing" as the polar opposite of the "left wing." Such simplistic definitions and neat dichotomies may carry some truth, but they hide more than they reveal. Specifically, they hide the modernness of fascism, its appeal to progressives and the avant-garde. Fascism has always been on the cutting edge.

It is particularly important to know, precisely, why the Nazis hated the Jews. Racism alone cannot explain the virulence of Nazi anti-Semitism. What did they see in the Jews that they thought was so inferior? What was the Jewish legacy that, in their mind, so poisoned Western culture? What were the Aryan ideals that the Nazis sought to restore, once the Jews and their influence were purged from Western culture?

The fascists aligned themselves not only against the Jews but against what the Jews contributed to Western civilization. A transcendent God, who reveals a transcendent moral law, was anathema to the fascists. Such transcendence, they argued, alienates human beings from nature and from themselves. Fascist intellectuals sought

13

to forge a new spirituality of immanence, focused upon nature, human emotions, and the community. The fascists sought to restore the ancient pre-Christian consciousness, the ancient mythic sensibility, in which individuals experience unity with nature, with each other, and with their own deepest impulses.

Fascism was essentially a spiritual movement. It was a revolt against the Judeo-Christian tradition, that is to say, against the Bible. Some fascists believed that Christianity could be purged of its Jewish elements; others believed it should be completely replaced. Some advocated a syncretistic Christianity, revising the faith to make it accord with the new culture. Others sought completely different kinds of religious experience. The fascist rebellion against transcendence restored the ancient pagan consciousness. With it came barbarism, a barbarism armed with modern technology and intellectual sophistication. The liquidation of the transcendent moral law and "Jewish" conscience allowed the resurgence of the most primitive and destructive emotions, the unleashing of original sin.

This book is a study of 20th-century fascism, before, during, and after Hitler. There is a continuity in 20th-century thought, of which fascism is an important and often neglected part. I will be exploring the connection between fascism and existentialism, theological liberalism, and the avant-garde. My goal is to present the ideas of the fascist theorists from the inside, to make clear their internal logic and the reasons for their appeal. My method is a perhaps unusual combination of historical narrative, cultural criticism, and theological analysis. Despite my criticisms of postmodern ideology, this book is something of an exercise in postmodern scholarship.

I expect this work to be controversial, but those who question what I say about fascist ideology and its modern context may consult the wealth of recent scholarship on fascism, World War II, and the Holocaust. The work of the specialists, analyzing primary sources and sifting through historical evidence, deserves urgent study and application. Robert Lifton's *The Nazi Doctors* should be required reading for those involved in the controversies of medical ethics. Church historians such as Robert Ericksen, Franklin Littell, and Ernst Helmreich need to be studied when seminaries address the question of the relationship between Christ and culture. Although he has come under criticism by Holocaust scholars for some of his Heideggerian tendencies, Ernst Nolte's phenomenological analysis of fascism is a valuable resource, as is Zeev Sternhell's historical study of the origins of fascism. Victor Farias's biography of Heidegger not only reveals controversial facts about the great philosopher, but vividly recreates the academic climate in Hitler's Germany. Jewish authors such as George Steiner, Max Weinreich, and Elie Wiesel were invaluable in helping me to formulate my thesis. The literature of the Holocaust looms as an inexhaustible resource for the study of the human condition, and I am grateful to David Hirsch, with his eloquent polemics against postmodernist evasions, for underscoring that fact.

Thanks as always goes to my family, especially my wife Jackquelyn. I would also like to acknowledge my friends, students, and colleagues with whom I have tried out these ideas. David Berger, presently head librarian at Concordia Seminary in St. Louis, was particularly helpful in my research. I owe a special debt to my late colleague William Houser, to whom this book is dedicated. A communications scholar, Bill was the one who drew the contrast between the worldview implicit in Leni Riefenstahl's cinematic tribute to Hitler, "The Triumph of the Will," and that of Luther's "The Bondage of the Will." Our discussions helped to precipitate this project.

Thanks too should go to Wilbert Rosin, editor of Concordia Publishing House, who stretched some parameters and asked to publish this book. This is, in fact, an example of Lutheran scholarship. The Lutheran tradition is often blamed for Germany's easy capitulation to Hitler, so this attack against fascism may be seen as an act of penance (if Lutherans believed in penance). But I write not just as a Lutheran but as a *confessional* Lutheran, committed to Scripture and to doctrine, to the transcendent spirituality of historical Christianity that has been so under attack throughout the century. I hope I am in the tradition, not of the syncretists, but of the confessional Lutherans in Hitler's Germany who stood up against the times and gave their lives for their faith.

1

"A Disease of the Times" Introduction

By killing the Jews, Western culture would eradicate those who had "invented" God. . . . The Holocaust is a reflex, the more complete for being long inhibited, of natural sensory consciousness, of instinctual polytheistic and animist needs.

—George Steiner[1]

This book is an attempt to probe what David H. Hirsch has described as "the dark secret that European high culture in its most advanced phase not only was powerless to prevent the construction and implementation of the death camps, but actually provided the ideological base on which the death camps were built."[2] An even darker secret is that the very same "advanced phase" of modern thought that brought us the death camps has continued to advance in the same direction, as if nothing had ever happened.

Thomas Mann, the German novelist who knew but ultimately resisted the seduction of fascism, has called it "a disease of the times which is at home everywhere and from which no country is free."[3] Even after Hitler's defeat, Mann continued to refer to "the fascist era of the Occident in which we live and, despite the military victory over fascism, will long continue to live."[4]

The defeat of Hitler and the Axis powers in World War II meant the military defeat of fascism, but an ideology cannot be defeated by military power alone. Ideas linger. They are reborn when the time is right again, or they come out of hiding in strange new shapes. The major scandal of contemporary thought is that, despite World War and Holocaust, the intellectual heritage of fascism has never been repudiated.

Oddly enough, few people today have a clear idea of exactly what it is that fascists believe. Fascism is not merely the seizure of

16

power by madmen. It is certainly not conservatism. Nor can it be understood simply as racism, totalitarianism, or "right wing extremism." These may be symptoms, but they are not the essence of the disease. Fascism is a worldview.

The elements of this worldview derive from romanticism, Darwinism, and existentialism. They are part of the mainstream of Western thought. As such, they were basic assumptions of the intellectual elite of the 1930s. They remain so today.

This worldview soon acquired spiritual implications. Fascist totalitarianism was more than a system of political control; it was totalitarian in seeking to encompass and to direct all of life. Fascism emerged not only as a political and economic system but as a new religion, whose promise was to heal the alienation of the modern world. The emotional life would be freed, harmony with nature would be achieved, and the culture would be revitalized. This new worldview defined itself against the existing spiritual framework—that of the Jews and their Bible. In rejecting not only the Bible but objective meaning, transcendent morality, and the authority of language itself, the fascists arrayed themselves against the Word.

The Theology of Fascism

Fascism can be understood most clearly in terms of its archenemy, the Jew. Just as the Nazis sought to exterminate the Jews, fascism sought to eliminate the Judeo-Christian tradition from Western culture.

Ernst Nolte has defined fascism as "the practical and violent resistance to transcendence."[5] Whereas the Judeo-Christian tradition focuses on a transcendent God and a transcendent moral law, fascist spirituality is centered upon what is tangible. Nature and the community assume the mystical role they held in the ancient mythological religions. Religious zeal is displaced away from the transcendent onto the immanent: the land, the people, the blood, the will.

Fascists seek an organic, neomythological unity of nature, the community, and the self. The concepts of a God who is above nature and a moral law that is above society are rejected. Such transcendent beliefs are alienating, cutting off human beings from their natural existence and from each other.

17

Specifically, such transcendent beliefs were condemned as being "Jewish." Fascist anti-Semitism was not merely racial—despite the biological race theory that dominated National Socialism. The rationale for anti-Semitism was also the *ideas* of the Jews. According to fascist theorists, the Jewish influence—that is, the idea of a transcendent religion and a transcendent moral law—was responsible for the ills of Western culture. The target of the fascists was not only the Jews but the Judeo-Christian tradition.

Christianity was to be purged of the Bible. Because Christianity has always been open to culture, there have always been versions of Christianity that lend themselves to becoming absorbed by the culture. Most fascists saw the need of organized religion to give a sacred status to visible social institutions. This might be accomplished under the form of a romanticized Catholicism or the civil religion of Protestantism. Liberal theology, which originated in prewar Germany, challenged the church's traditional preoccupation with transcendent issues such as the salvation of the soul. Instead, it gave the church new, this-worldly agendas centering on culture and politics. Biblical criticism as practiced by the liberal theologians weakened the authority of the Bible, and thus diminished the "Jewish" presence within Christianity.

Although fascism was willing to accept Christianity insofar as it could be transformed into a state nature-religion, the more radical factions sought the restoration of the pre-Christian tribal religions. What the fascist religious reforms really amounted to was the establishment of a primitivistic neopaganism. The fascists sought to recover the mythological consciousness, which brought nature, the culture, and the psyche into a unity. Casting off the Judeo-Christian tradition, as codified in the Hebraic scriptures, did not bring on a new spiritual order. Instead, it resulted in a resurgence of the most primitive spirituality—the old pagan order of the divine-king, the sacred community, the communion with nature, and the sacrifices of blood.

Fascism represented a revival of ancient pagan culture over against the Judeo-Christian tradition. The fascists glorified the primitive, as we do now. The mythological cultures may have promoted psychic integration, communal unity, and harmony with the environment. But they also demanded strict conformity to the group, made social criticism impossible, glorified war, and allowed such

18

brutal practices as infanticide and euthanasia.[6] Both these positive and these negative points of mythological cultures were realized in fascism.

Today, neopaganism is coming back into vogue. In the religion sections of the book store chains, books on astrology, fortune-telling, and the occult crowd out Judeo-Christian books. The New Age movement is reviving ancient pagan practices such as attending to oracles (channelers) and sacred objects (crystals). In Christianity, both conservative and liberal churches are shifting their attention away from a transcendent focus. Instead of prophetic judgment and the offer of salvation, many churches are proclaiming a this-worldly gospel. Political activism, whether of the left or the right, is consuming the energy of American Christianity. Both liberals and conservatives are downplaying transcendent doctrines in favor of subjective experience and the emotional fulfillment that comes from losing one's identity in a larger group. What Ernst Nolte describes as "the resistance to transcendence" is characterizing contemporary religion, as well as the culture as a whole.

Fascism and Modern Thought

Martin Heidegger, who may be the most sophisticated and influential philosopher of the 20th century, we now know was an active, ideologically committed Nazi. Recent revelations about the extent of Heidegger's Nazism[7] have proven embarrassing and bewildering to his followers. It seems outrageous that someone with a mind like Heidegger's could succumb to Adolf Hitler's party line. Heidegger may have been an opportunist, some are saying, but his political activities should not be allowed to detract from his philosophical contributions. His existentialism should not be discredited by the ad hominem attack. That there may be a genuine connection between Heidegger's existentialism and the ideology of National Socialism is almost impossible for many people to consider.

When it was discovered that the postmodern critic Paul De Man had been a propagandist for a pro-Nazi periodical, his followers were plunged into confusion.[8] Surely De Man's methodology of deconstruction can have nothing to do with fascism. Deconstruction throws all objective meaning and all authority into question. As such, it must be a defense against fascism. Whatever De Man did in his

19

youth in occupied Belgium, the reasoning goes, should by no means discredit his intellectual contribution. It seems almost unthinkable that deconstruction and fascism may be related.

Whether or not Heidegger and De Man were naive in their allegiance to fascism, the controversy about their involvement does show the naivete of contemporary scholarship. It is as if the memory of fascism—what it was and why it was so appealing—has been suppressed from our cultural consciousness.

Heidegger and De Man were by no means alone in their enthusiasm for Mussolini and Hitler. As Stephen Spender has admitted, "some of the greatest modern writers sympathized with fascism."[9] Spender cites Ezra Pound, D. H. Lawrence, and W. B. Yeats. Alastair Hamilton, in his book *The Appeal of Fascism: A Study of Intellectuals and Fascism, 1919–1945,* discusses these writers and adds to their company George Bernard Shaw, Wyndham Lewis, T. E. Hulme, Roy Campbell, and the early T. S. Eliot. Avant-garde artistic movements—Vorticists, Italian Futurists, German Expressionists—included many devotees of fascism.

We could add prominent and influential figures from other fields. Carl Jung, the psychiatrist and advocate of mythological consciousness, flirted at least briefly with fascism.[10] Margaret Sanger, founder of Planned Parenthood, promoted Hitler's eugenics program in the United States.[11]

The list of fascist sympathizers reads like a *Who's Who* of 20th-century culture. To be sure, many of them recanted their earlier allegiance once the war broke out and the horrific implications of fascism became clear. Nevertheless, they made up the intellectual and cultural climate that brought Hitler into power.

Fascism is a major element of 20th-century thought and culture. To suppress this truth is to evade history. Fascism cannot be understood apart from its connections to the mainstream of modern culture. Conversely, 20th-century thought cannot be understood apart from its connections to fascism.

The pro-Nazi modernists continue to be influential. Ezra Pound has continued to influence modern literature. It did not matter to poets or critics that he was a fascist. Heidegger is still revered in universities and in theological seminaries. His allegiance to Adolf Hitler has not detracted from his popularity among intellectuals and theologians. The ways of thinking and the cultural trends which precipitated the Nazi horrors did not go away just because Hitler died in a bunker. Indeed, as the memory of Hitler fades, they are more and more coming back into vogue.

Robert Casillo has studied how scholars treat Ezra Pound's fascism. No one can deny Pound's virulent anti-Semitism and his propaganda broadcasts for Mussolini. Still, most critics downplay his fascism. They focus instead on what they see as Pound's more positive contributions to 20th-century culture. They study Pound's antimonotheism, his agrarianism, his neopaganism, his glorification of myth, his love of nature, his insistence on the concrete and suspicion of the abstract. Such aspects of Pound's writings, treated in isolation, are presented as progressive and humane.

What most Pound scholars apparently do not realize is that these values all come from fascism. Antimonotheism, agrarianism, neopaganism, mythological consciousness, nature mysticism, antirationalism, and related positions "taken together form a typical, mutually reinforcing fascist constellation."[12] Such beliefs—even more than his broadcasts for Mussolini—constitute his fascism. Yet contemporary scholars praise them, oblivious that they are praising fascism. That scholars find these ideas progressive and humane is proof that the intellectual climate is still naively open to fascism.

To implicate today's intellectual establishment with fascism would seem to be absurd on the face of it. There are few if any members of the Klan, the White Aryan Nation, or other ultraright hate groups on university faculties. The academic culture, on the contrary, tends to favor the left. Marxism may be fashionable, but never fascism. Among our intellectual elite, racism is universally deplored. Authoritarianism of every kind is questioned. The new political activism on college campuses asserts the rights of women and minority groups and attempts to root out every vestige of oppression. Even if a connection could be shown between fascism and deconstruction, it could hardly change the fact that deconstructive critics are radical, not reactionary.

But if the modernist thinkers were naive in unwittingly opening the Pandora's box of fascism, postmodernist thinkers should beware of the same naivete. A set of ideas is emerging from today's academic world that is startlingly reminiscent of what the fascist theorists were saying in the 1930s: individual identity is a myth, insofar as identity is really determined by culture and ethnicity; laws and social con-

21

ventions are only masks for power; human-centered values are part of a corrupt Western civilization; the transcendent meaning of reason, objectivity, and language is an illusion. Is it possible that those who hold these views do not realize that these are also the doctrines of fascism?

Those who reject the concept of individual identity as a myth and believe that all reality is socially constructed should consider the political implications of what they are saying. With those assumptions, can there be such a thing as individual freedom? Can there be any limits on the power of the state?

Those who assert that all laws, governments, relationships, and institutions are nothing more than patterns of oppression and masks for the raw exercise of power should realize that these assumptions cut both ways. A power reductionist may uncover injustices and take the side of the oppressed. A power reductionist could just as easily justify repression as inevitable and rationalize the unrestrained use of power.

Those who assault Western civilization in favor of ethnicity, primitivism, environmentalism, and subjectivism should realize that their critiques and the alternatives they present are almost identical to those made by the theorists of fascism. Those who gleefully deconstruct "humanistic values" should wonder what sorts of values will take their place. What would a "new morality" that is "nonhumanistic" look like? Might it resemble what we now call evil?

Today's postmodernists criticize "humanistic" values in what they consider a liberating way. They attack the concept of individual identity to restore a sense of social responsibility. They uncover the hidden workings of power to expose oppression based on race, gender, or class. They have the best of motives. They are certainly not fascists.

And yet, they need to realize that the fascists of the 1930s also sought to dismantle Western civilization and its human-centered values. They too attacked the concept of individual identity and taught that reality is socially constructed. They too insisted that underlying all institutions is naked power. They too prized ethnicity. They too were environmentalists. They too questioned the objectivity of meaning.

The difference is that contemporary thinkers in this vein bemoan the structures of power and oppression that they uncover. They still work with unexamined moral assumptions, overlooking the way they have demolished the basis of those assumptions.

The fascists, on the other hand, took these assumptions to their logical conclusions. If individual autonomy is an illusion, then everyone should find identity in the communal state. If society shapes the individual, then let it do so, replacing individual liberty with propaganda and social control. If power underlies all social institutions, then let us exercise power. If race and ethnicity is a determining value, then ideas should be evaluated in racial and ethnic terms. If societies are intrinsically racist, with one ethnic group oppressing the others, then let us be racist, protecting our racial identity in this power struggle by subjugating the other races.

Surely few if any postmodern thinkers would go this far. My concern is not so much with the current intellectual scene as it is with what might come next. What will the "post-contemporary" movement look like, once the postmodernists have successfully discredited objectivity, freedom, and morality? What sort of society will be erected on the rubble, once the Western tradition is deconstructed? Most of the modernist proto-fascists shrank back in horror when they saw the consequences of their ideas as acted out by Adolf Hitler. My concern is that today's postmodernists may be likewise unleashing a demon.

As David Hirsch has pointed out, the ostensible goals of postmodernists—equal rights for women and minorities, social and economic justice—derive from Judeo-Christian and democratic values and predate deconstructionism. They can not be derived from deconstruction alone, which cannot give a conceptual base for human rights and individual freedom.[13]

> Although the postmodernists claim to be critical of the social ills of contemporary life—runaway technology and technocracy, the power of the state, capitalism, imperialism, colonialism, oppression of the downtrodden (all of which have been targets of respectable pre-postmodern liberal criticism as well)—their ideology carries with it, inevitably, the less desirable tendencies of their patron saint, Heidegger [:] Their attack on the Cartesian human subject and on reason itself; their contempt for the values of liberalism, of human and individual rights, and of constitutional democracy, ... their depreciation of human values (which they

23

prefer to call bourgeois values) and their mocking of any notion
of "transcendence."[14]

Such postmodern notions are not only Heideggerian, they are specifically fascist.

Today, explicit fascism of the old school has returned. The collapse of communism has spawned new cults of national socialism. Race and ethnicity are once again central issues, from Belgrade to Los Angeles. Neo-Nazi groups such as the White Aryan Nation grow into subcultures, especially among white prison inmates. Anti-Semitism is back. Skinheads hand out fascist literature on street corners and in schools. Neo-Nazi parties gain political power in Europe and stage riots in which non-European immigrants are killed.

Such extremist organizations, particularly with their appeal to young people, are dangerous; but the more subtle and widespread trends with parallels to fascism may be even more dangerous. An aesthetics of violence—which has clear affinities to the Nazi aesthetic—is dominating both the work of serious artists and that of popular filmmakers. Avant-garde critics are demolishing all objective values and meanings, reducing them, in the fascist way, to issues of sheer power. Irrationalism—a key feature of fascist ideology—remains an academic exercise, but it is now a characteristic of the whole culture.

The fascist dream of a mass consciousness, in which the individual is swallowed up into a greater whole by the power of propaganda, can now be realized by the impact of the mass media. The trivialization of our political discourse, the subjectivity and politicizing of religion, the decline of language before the visual image, and the collapse of moral objectivity may well foreshadow an emerging fascist worldview.

The slogan of the Holocaust survivors is "never again!" To keep such a pledge, it is necessary to recognize and to name those modes of thinking that, perhaps inadvertently, led to the Nazi atrocities. This must also involve recovering what the Nazis so hated in the Jews—an ethic and a worldview grounded in the transcendent Word.

2

"The Doctrine of Our Age" The Fascist Tradition

If each age has its doctrine, the innumerable symptoms indicate that the doctrine of our age is the Fascist one.

—Benito Mussolini[1]

Fascism has a distinguished pedigree. Its assumptions reach deep into the intellectual history of the West. It permeates modern culture, in the Left as well as the Right, among the avant-garde as well as among conservatives, in the popular culture as well as the lunatic fringe.

Fascism is difficult to recognize because it is so poorly understood and because its nature is masked behind collective denial. Although fascism had a coherent ideology, few people today can describe exactly what the fascists of the 1930s and 1940s stood for.

The label *fascist,* as Zeev Sternhell as observed, has become "*the* term of abuse par excellence, conclusive and unanswerable."[2] Calling someone a fascist is a way to insult and vilify an opponent. No one claims the label. Fascism is what people ascribe to their enemies, never to themselves. As the word is detached from what it signifies, the substance of fascism lives on, undetected because unnamed.

Fascism to most people is now little more than a symbol. Rather than a set of ideas, which may be accepted or rejected, fascism has become synonymous with archetypal evil. Fascists have become the all-purpose villains of popular culture.[3] The sadistic torturer, leering through his monocle, the malevolent goose-stepping clown, the monster who mindlessly follows orders by machine-gunning innocent people—these images of fascism dominate our imaginations. They obscure something even more frightening—that actual fascists could be very much like us.

Defenders of distinguished fascist intellectuals such as Martin

Heidegger and Paul De Man regularly cite what good and decent people they were, as if they were not real Nazis because they were so different from the Nazis in the movies. A person might be kindly, thoughtful, creative, intelligent, and still be a fascist. Books about thinkers who would prove influential to fascist theory—such as Nietzsche—and prominent modernists who were sympathetic to fascism—such as Ezra Pound—follow predictable patterns in skimming over the connections and making excuses about how their subject was deceived or misunderstood. David Hirsch has detected a pattern of evasion among Western intellectuals parallel to the denial of responsibility for the death camps among those who collaborated with the Nazis—"the concealment of a shameful European past that must be uncovered, always in the face of intense and hostile opposition."[4]

Right Wing and Left Wing

Part of the problem in recognizing fascism is the assumption that it is conservative. Sternhell has observed how study of the ideology has been obscured by "the official Marxist interpretation of fascism."[5] Marxism defines fascism as its polar opposite. If Marxism is progressive, fascism is conservative. If Marxism is left wing, fascism is right wing. If Marxism champions the proletariat, fascism champions the bourgeoisie. If Marxism is socialist, fascism is capitalist.

The influence of Marxist scholarship has severely distorted our understanding of fascism. Communism and fascism were rival brands of socialism. Whereas Marxist socialism is predicated on an international class struggle, fascist *national socialism* promoted a socialism centered in national unity. Both communists and fascists opposed the bourgeoisie. Both attacked the conservatives. Both were mass movements, which had special appeal for the intelligentsia, students, and artists, as well as workers. Both favored strong, centralized governments and rejected a free economy and the ideals of individual liberty. Fascists saw themselves as being neither of the right nor the left. They believed that they constituted a third force, synthesizing the best of both extremes.[6] There are important differences and bitter ideological enmity between Marxism and fascism; but their opposition to each other should not disguise their kinship as revolutionary socialist ideologies.

Nor should figures of speech such as *right wing* or *left wing,* or artificial constructs such as *reactionary* and *radical* obscure a way of thinking that permeated a whole range of political and social positions. The left wing/right wing metaphor, which portrays the two revolutionary ideologies as opposite extremes, is profoundly misleading. Jaroslav Krejci has shown the inadequacy of the "unilinear imagery" of left vs. right.[7] He points out that the metaphor comes from the seating arrangements in the French parliament after the Revolution. Politically, those seated on the right favored an absolute monarch. Economically, they favored government monopolies and a controlled economy. Culturally, they favored authoritarian control of the people. Those seated on the left favored democracy, a free market economy, and personal liberty.[8]

Such a spatial metaphor corresponded well to the Cartesian geometry[9] of the Enlightenment and to 18th-century political options, but it breaks down as a model for 20th-century politics. In terms of the original model, American conservatives who want less government and trust the free market would be on the *left*. Liberals who want more of a government-directed economy would be on the *right*.[10] *Liberal* and *conservative* are themselves relative terms— depending upon what one has to conserve. The *liberals* of the 19th century, with their free-market economics and resistance to government control, are the *conservatives* of the 20th century.

When it comes to socialist alternatives, as Krejci shows, the range of left and right becomes meaningless. Marxist states practice a controlled economy and have a strong, authoritative central government with strict controls upon their populations. They would have to sit in the *right wing* of the French parliament. On the other hand, Marxists are revolutionaries and thus definitely anticonservative. Fascist socialism, for all its differences with Marxism, is similar in advocating a controlled economy, a strong central government, and strict control over the populace, while being culturally and intellectually radical. Nevertheless, as Krejci says, "in spite of many affinities between them, the communists continued to be viewed as the extreme left and the Nazis as the supreme right."[11] As a result, those who think of themselves as being "politically correct" leftists accuse "right-wing" conservatives of being fascists, but are oblivious to fascist tendencies of their own.

Alienation

Fascism is essentially a response to the alienation that has been a part of the spiritual landscape of the West since the Enlightenment. Individuals in the modern world feel isolated from each other. Science, technology, and the economic realities and environmental damage of the industrial revolution isolate the individual from nature. There has thus been a genuine yearning for community and for an organic unity with the natural world.

Logic and rationalism, with their cold analyses and denial of basic human impulses, have seemed stifling, heightening the sense of alienation. If objective knowledge is alienating, subjective experience is liberating and healing. Authentic existence comes from unleashing the emotions, cultivating the subjective and irrational dimension of life. The attempts to resolve the dilemma of alienation, understandable as they are, would find concrete and political expression in fascism.[12]

The industrial revolution, which began in the 18th century and has continued to accelerate, meant a profound alteration in human life. Nature was replaced by the machine. The village was replaced by the factory. Before the industrial revolution, most people made their living from nature. The rhythms of nature—the seasons, the patterns of light and darkness, the sequence of seedtime and harvest—regulated their lives. With industrialization, this intimacy with nature was broken. The factories meant that people worked inside rather than outside. They could rely on manufactured goods rather than what they grew or made themselves. The advent of the machine freed people from their dependence upon nature, but at the cost of alienation from their environment.

With the rise of modern science, which accompanied the industrial revolution, nature itself began to be seen as a machine. Nature was interpreted as a closed system of cause and effect, which can be totally explained by mathematical and experimental analysis. Whereas preindustrial human beings confronted nature as a mysterious living organism, the scientists of the Enlightenment reduced nature to a complex but inert mechanism that could be taken apart, rationally understood, and used like any other mechanical device.

The machine dominated, exploited, and violated nature. Tracts of hills and forests were leveled. Raw materials were dug out of the earth, fed into the machines, and transformed into products for human consumption. Industrial waste fouled the air, the water, and the landscape. Already by the turn of the 19th century, William Blake was condemning the "dark Satanic Mills" that were polluting the air and blackening the churches.[13] A hundred years later, Gerard Manley Hopkins, writing about nature, complained that "all is seared with trade; bleared, smeared with toil;/And wears man's smudge and shares man's smell: the soil is bare now."[14]

Industrialism not only altered human beings' relationship with nature, it also revolutionized social relationships. Small family farms were combined in the name of industrial efficiency into huge tracts of land that were worked by machines. Displaced farmers poured into the cities, where they worked in factories, servicing machines. The close communal ties of village life were replaced by the impersonal economic ties of the big city. Extended families that had been rooted in one place for generations were broken up, with family members moving wherever they could find a job. In the old agricultural village, each member of the nuclear family had a distinct and important role, with the father, mother, and children taking their places in a stable social and economic order. In the early industrial cities, men, women, and even children tended the factories, working long hours at subsistence wages. Traditional family life among the poor was shattered.

Social alienation was also fueled by the rise of democracy. Although democracy, like industrialism, was in many ways liberating, it was also destabilizing. The democratic reforms accompanied the Enlightenment and shared its rationalistic assumptions. The centuries-old hierarchies, in which everyone had a clearly defined role, were toppled by the new ideology of equality. One's identity, formerly determined by class and family, became uncertain. Old bonds of custom were replaced by an impersonal legal code. The democratic revolution and its ideology of individualism and equality questioned all traditional authorities, resulting in confusion and cynicism. The organic unity of the old order—in which individuals were united into the larger organism of family, community, and nation—was replaced by competing factions and by competing individuals, each pursuing a narrow self-interest. The old sense of belonging, of being a part of a greater whole, was lost.

Romanticism

People felt alienated from nature, from society, and—because their identity had become such an enigma—from themselves. The rationalism of the Enlightenment, which seemed responsible for this malaise, was answered in the 19th century by *Romanticism.*

The romantics reasserted the value of the natural world. Nature was not seen as a machine, but as a living organism. Nature is not to be approached merely by the analyzing intellect, by which, as Wordsworth complains, "we murder to dissect."[15] By contemplating the beauties and sublimities of nature, we can experience a oneness with the universe that can bring healing and inspiration.

The romantics' apotheosis of nature was accompanied by a new assertion of the self. Passion, not reason, is uniquely "natural." Disdaining the artificiality of abstract intellect, the romantics cultivated concrete experiences and genuine emotions. Romantic subjectivism and antirationalism were bolstered by philosophical analysis. Kant and his followers argued that knowledge of the objective world is problematic, that all we can be certain of are mental sensations. Kant dismantled the Enlightenment's empiricism by demonstrating how the human mind actively shapes the data from the senses. The self becomes not only a passive receiver of information but an active shaper of its world.

Romanticism was also characterized by nostalgia for the past and admiration for the primitive. An important paradigm for Romanticism is "the noble savage," who, unspoiled by the trappings of a more sophisticated society, lives in unity with nature. Primitive cultures are thus morally superior to advanced and alienated civilizations. Romantics searched their own heritage, collecting folktales, writing historical novels, and cultivating a new nationalism based upon ethnic identity.

Many romantics responded to alienation by revelling in the isolation of the individual. Scorning society, they found consolation in nature and in their personal quests for self-fulfillment. Yet Romanticism did have political implications. Jean Jacques Rousseau, the first theorist of Romanticism, synthesized individual liberty with his idea of the state as a collective organism in his concept of "the general will," which can be embodied in a single leader.[16] The French Revolution began as an Enlightenment exercise in the *Rights of Man,* but the bloodletting of the Reign of Terror was romantic in its outpouring of passion and its unleashing of primitive emotions. The short-lived Republic was replaced by Napoleon, a romantic hero who embodied in himself the collective will of an awakened nationalism.

Romantic Materialism

In the latter part of the 19th century, the romantic view of nature and the self would be darkened. The research of Charles Darwin and Sigmund Freud challenged the sometimes facile optimism of the romantics. The early romantics believed that nature taught lessons of harmony and peace, that if people would only follow the moral example of nature that all would be well. Nature as revealed by Charles Darwin, however, is very different. Nature does not teach harmony and peace, but strife and violence. The law of nature is the survival of the fittest. Progress comes from ruthless competition, the strong destroying the weak. Nature, according to Tennyson, is "red in tooth and claw."[17]

Darwin's theory of evolution by natural selection had implications far beyond biology. What is true for nature must be true for the individual and society. If nature progresses by competition, struggle, and the victory of the strong over the weak, all progress must come in the same way. This seemed to hold true in the economy, with the dramatic success of 19th-century cutthroat capitalism. "As the notion of social Darwinism gained widespread acceptance," according to Sternhell, "it stripped the human personality of its sacramental dignity. It made no distinction between the physical life and the social life, and conceived of the human condition in terms of an unceasing struggle, whose natural outcome was the survival of the fittest."[18]

For scientists, Darwinism raised more questions and spawned new avenues of research. Sternhell cites how scientific positivism "felt the impact of social Darwinism, and underwent a profound change. In the latter half of the century its emphasis on deliberate and rational choice as the determining factor in human behavior gave way to new notions of heredity, race, and environment."[19] The concept of determinism further weakened democratic assumptions of liberty and equality. Some biologists, assuming that human beings

31

are nothing more than a species of animals, began examining races as subspecies. The spurious science of racialism, on the analogy of Darwinism, began to study competition between the races and race superiority. Social reformers sought to improve the species by formulating theories of eugenics.

Such a bleak and materialistic view of nature would seem to challenge romantic idealism and to increase the sense of alienation from nature. Many people abandoned Romanticism in light of Darwinism, and, like Tennyson, turned back to Christianity. Some romantics, though, were able to embrace Darwinism. It appealed to a certain elitism that was inherent in romantic individualism. Romantics tended to consider themselves superior beings in a world of mediocrities. The tough-mindedness of Darwinism, its sanction of ruthlessness, also could appeal to those romantics who were repelled by Victorian moralism and sentimentality. Their goal was still to become one with nature, even a nature red in tooth and claw.

As nature was being reinterpreted, Freud was forcing a reinterpretation of the self. Just as Darwin saw violent conflict as the essence of nature, Freud saw violent conflict as the essence of the self. Freud's exploration of the inner life was related to the self-exploration encouraged by Romanticism. Psychoanalysis taught that human behavior is dominated by subconscious, irrational forces.[20] Rationality is revealed to be nothing more than a thin veneer that papers over a riot of primitive passions. The guilt-inducing laws of the superego suppress the natural instincts, which a healthy personality must release. Freud's emphasis on sexuality may have been shocking, but it appealed strongly to the libertine strain in Romanticism. A Freudian view of sex seemed to justify a new morality based on the fulfillment of suppressed desires. These desires, according to Freud, are accompanied by violent and perverse impulses—yearnings for power, destruction, and death.

Whereas traditional morality stresses control of the passions, Freudianism delegitimizes the mechanisms of control and sanctions the unleashing of the passions. Whereas traditional morality values peace and compassion, Darwinism sanctions struggle and violence as the mechanisms for progress. Both thinkers, in addressing the two romantic poles of nature and the self, made possible a new kind of scientific materialism. The science of the Enlightenment tended to promote reason, equality, and freedom, all of which could be supported through the rational design of democratic institutions. The new materialism, on the other hand, undermined all of the assumptions of democracy. As Sternhell observes,

> The new theories of social and political psychology rejected out of hand the traditional mechanistic concept of man, which asserted that human behavior is governed by rational choice. Opinion now dictated that sentiment and feeling count for more in political questions than reasoning, and fostered contempt for democracy and its institutions and workings.[21]

The key figure in the emergence of a romantic materialism that would embrace both Darwinian science and philosophical irrationalism was Friedrich Nietzsche. His critique of compassion and glorification of violence, his belief in the evolution of a Superman who would be beyond good and evil, and his intellectual assault on the Judeo-Christian tradition were foundation stones in the development of fascist theory. Nietzsche's ideas—important as they are both for fascism and for contemporary thought—will be discussed in more detail in subsequent chapters. Suffice it to say that with Darwin, Freud, and Nietzsche, the elements of the fascist worldview were in place.

By the 1890s, the intellectual climate of Europe was saturated with Darwinism, race theories, and philosophical irrationalism. The "new" intellectuals of the day, according to Sternhell, attacked rationalistic individualism and the breaking of communal ties; attacked cities with their deadening routines; and attacked claims of reason in favor of instinct, "sometimes even of animality."[22] The typical responses to the alienation of the times were movements of revolt: "Revolt against the world of matter and reason, against materialism and positivism, against the mediocrity of bourgeois society, against the muddle of liberal democracy."[23] The fashion for young intellectuals—as it is today—was "to impeach Western civilization itself, which in their eyes was fundamentally corrupt."[24]

Such views became commonplace, not only among the intellectual elite but among students and journalists, popular novelists and the general educated public.[25] Ordinary people became acclimated to these lines of thinking. They were conditioned to accept the idea of a new morality and a new social order.[26]

In the aftermath of World War I, the economic collapse of the 1930s, and the apparent failure of democracy to deal with these problems, the alienation that was a product of the modern world reached crisis proportions. By then, the theoretical framework of the new movement was complete and had coalesced into a political movement.

Fascist parties sprang up in nearly all of the nations of Europe. That they were to have their most dramatic success in Germany was no accident. As Robert Ericksen has observed, the crisis of modernity climaxed in the Weimar Republic, which was the center of psycho-analysis, the new relativistic physics, untrammeled industrialism, and modern theology.[27]

Nationalism Plus Socialism

The fascist parties offered not only a philosophy but a specific political and economic program. An early definition summed up their program in a simple formula: "Nationalism + Socialism = Fascism."[28]

Marxist socialism is international in scope, grounded in the universal struggle between those who own the means of production and the workers whom they exploit. For Marx, nations are an artificial construction of the bourgeoisie, a mechanism of laws and mystification designed for social control. True socialism will come when "the workers of the *world* unite" to throw off their economic masters.

National socialism, on the other hand, stresses national solidarity, not class struggle.[29] The goal is national unity, a collective in which everyone cooperates in their own roles for the national good. Fascists criticize Marxists for minimizing the cultural and communal ties that define a nation. For fascists, Marxism is too similar to capitalism. Both reduce human life to economic terms and are grounded in scientific rationalism.[30]

Capitalism was the first target of fascism, specifically "banking capitalism."[31] The problem is not that capitalism encourages the accumulation of private property, but that capitalism is based wholly on money. Actual tangible goods are less important than "capital." The banks control investment and thereby direct the economy. The high finance of the banks manipulates the economy and exploits everyone.

This is because banks make money not by producing something of value but by charging interest. Private property does not really belong to the people but to those who hold the mortgages. Charging interest means that everyone's productive labor is going into the pockets of the financiers. Workers, farmers, small businessmen, factory owners—all are enslaved by the banks. This view of capitalism was then linked with anti-Semitism, building on the perception that the financial sector of the economy was controlled by Jews.

Fascism stresses accession to property, not expropriation. Workers should share company profits.[32] Instead of a free market, with everyone competing selfishly with each other, the economy should be controlled and directed by the state for the common good.

Whereas capitalism stresses competition between individuals and Marxism stresses competition between social classes, fascist economic theory stresses competition between nations. According to Enrico Corradi, an early theorist of Italian fascism, "Just as [Marxist] socialism taught the proletariat the value of the class struggle, we must teach Italy the value of the international struggle."[33] Taking up the Marxist terminology, fascist economists portrayed Italy as a proletariat *nation*, exploited by the wealthier countries.[34] Nationalistic competition meant protectionist trade policies.[35] "The international struggle" would later be expressed in war.

Radicals of the time switched easily between Marxist and fascist brands of socialism, demonstrating once more the fallacy that they were as opposed to each other as "left" and "right." Henri de Man, president of the Belgian Workers' Party, switched from a class-based socialism to a national socialism. He became an important fascist theorist and has been described as "one of the most original socialist philosophers of the 20th century."[36] He was the uncle of the deconstructionist critic Paul De Man.

Although the particulars of fascist economic theory are not heard very often, one could argue that most modern socialism follows the model of national socialism rather than that of Marx. It has been observed that the economic policies of Franklin Roosevelt, geared to pulling America out of the recession by federal intervention into the economy, were very similar to those of Mussolini.[37] The socialism

35

of the European welfare states is perhaps a benign, tamed version of national socialism.

Even the communism of the former Soviet Union, in practice, was less an international movement of workers than a national socialism. The figure of Stalin—Hitler's counterpart as the absolute leader of a totalitarian state—makes the comparison very close indeed. In today's postcommunist Russia, free-market economic reforms are opposed by new authoritarian, nationalistic parties whose members are ex-Marxists and whose ideology is national socialism.

Today's politically-correct intellectuals, although they may think of themselves as being *leftist* or even *Marxist,* show little class consciousness. They certainly do not identify with blue-collar workers. They believe in economic justice, but they seldom want to eliminate private property altogether. Rather than seeing the middle class as the villains, they have conspiracy theories about the "multinational corporations." They tend to analyze the economy in terms of groups—blacks, Hispanics, whites, women—rather than in terms of individual competition or class distinctions. The more radical among them seek a social transformation; they do not, however, usually look to the collapse of capitalism and the revolt of the working class, but to the birth of a new order based on unity and harmony. In all these ways, they are closer to Henri de Man, and to Mussolini, than they are to Marx.

The Folkish State

Fascist economic theory addresses the problem of alienation by positing a unified, collective economy. The people of the nation find fulfillment in assuming their varying economic roles, without exploiting or competing with each other. People receive the tangible fruits of their own labor—actual property, as opposed to the abstraction of wealth as represented in the complex mathematics of banking capitalism. National Socialism, however, was more than an economic program. It was an ideology encompassing all of life.

The fascist critique of individualism is, according to Zeev Sternhell, "the cornerstone of fascist social and political thought."[38] In this view, there is no such thing as an autonomous identity. "The notion that man exists in perfect freedom anterior or exterior to society is simply a fiction."[39] The individual human being is "nothing

36

more than the vehicle of forces generated by the community."[40]

Such a view is precisely that of postmodern critical theorists. This is the ideological link between Henri de Man and his nephew, between the early fascist intellectuals and their contemporary successors. A common theme in postmodernist criticism is "the dissolution of the self"—claiming that the individual is a "fiction," a creation of bourgeois ideology.[41] Postmodernists "deconstruct the subject" by attempting to show that human consciousness itself is constituted by social forces and structures of power as embodied in language. The self cannot escape the "prison-house of language," through which the culture encodes itself and determines the very structure of what one is able to think.

Just as the postmodernists attack "humanism" on these grounds, the fascists also attacked human-centered values, including the concept of individual rights.[42] Since the culture determines the individual, the needs of the culture must have priority. According to the fascists, "The individual had no autonomy and only achieved the status of a human being as a member of a community."[43] Sternhell's summary of fascist ideology is today being echoed by apologists for abortion who argue, for example, that a child does not have the right to live until it is wanted by its mother and accepted by the human community.

Although this line of thought would develop into the conceptual justification for the death camps, the privileging of the community over the individual was not seen at the time as being purposefully inhumane. Rather, it was an insight that would eliminate the crisis of alienation. An individual can find fulfillment by becoming one with the group. The mass rallies, uniforms, and parades so favored by the early fascist parties were all mechanisms for creating group identity, giving people the experience of losing themselves by becoming part of a larger collective existence. Thus their loneliness and alienation would be healed.[44]

If the culture is at the root of the individual's identity and meaning, then the culture must acquire a mystical, even God-like status. Fascists made a point of distinguishing between *culture* and *civilization. Culture* was organic and ethnic, calling to mind the rural, agrarian life that was close to nature. *Civilization,* on the other hand, was mechanical and rational, calling to mind the city with its machines and its alienation. Culture was good; civilization was bad.

Culture created a sense of ethnic identity. Civilization, with its laws and denatured institutions, was "Jewish."[45] Fascists sought to undermine the sophisticated rationalism of Western civilization with its Enlightenment politics and its Judeo-Christian values. In its place, they sought to resurrect the more primitive and communal ideals of the pre-Christian Greeks, Romans, and Germanic tribes.[46]

In the traditions of liberal democracy, one's cultural background was at best a matter of sentimental attachment and at worst a hindrance to individual self-realization. The stifling conservatism of the old folkways was something to transcend. Many immigrants to the United States wanted to escape their cultures and to forge an identity of their own. Education and rational choices could allow anyone, theoretically at least, to participate in a society grounded in freedom and equality. The democratic ideal, in a sense, was a-cultural, or perhaps metacultural. Democratic nations were built not on cultural identity, nor on ethnicity, but upon a rational plan—such as the United States Constitution. Such a plan typically ruled out discrimination or favoritism based on cultural origin. In the United States, this official tolerance allowed for a true cultural pluralism, but it also pushed culture into the background, making it a matter of private ties rather than public identity. Rights and privileges were given to individuals, not cultures.

To be sure, this theory of individual equality and the de-emphasis upon ethnicity and culture did not always work in practice. The American institution of slavery based on race and the continued discrimination against blacks most blatantly contradicted the democratic ideal. In Europe, among many people, democracy's denial of culture and the downplaying of communal ties were seen as profoundly alienating. Much of the appeal of fascism was in its restoration of ethnic and cultural identity.

The glorification of culture and ethnicity, of course, led to racism. The major difference between Mussolini's Fascism and Hitler's Nation Socialism was their emphasis upon race. Mussolini, while upholding cultural determinism, rejected the idea that culture was a function of race. Hitler, on the other hand, embraced biological and racial determinism.[47] Hitler's racism was part of his Darwinism and his Romanticism, his desire to ground culture in what he saw as the natural order.

Today, culture is once again placed on center stage. Contemporary "multiculturalism" is, of course, very different from the fascist model of superior cultures lording it over inferior ones. Contemporary thought values pluralism and diversity, but it is a diversity not of individuals but of groups. Today's multiculturalism encourages the view that identity is a matter of ethnicity and culture rather than individual personality. The assumption is that culture determines one's identity. Individualism and the other traditional values of liberal democracy are seen not as a transcultural framework for a pluralistic society, but as more culturally-bound values peculiar to America.

The contemporary stress upon cultural identity is accompanied by sustained critiques of "Western civilization" in favor of cultural and ethnic consciousness. Primitive or tribal cultures are presented as being more virtuous than those "contaminated by Western civilization" and modern technology. American culture becomes guilty of "cultural imperialism," it is argued, by seeking to destroy the cultural identity of other groups by making them assimilate to democratic values.

Another important component of fascist ideology, with surprising links to contemporary thought, is *environmentalism*. Because of their Romanticism, fascists sought to overcome the alienation between the human being and nature. Again, the villain was modern civilization, with its scientific technology and polluting factories. Fascists believed that the soul of a culture is tied to the land from which it emerged.[48] Sternhell summarizes the tenets of fascist environmentalism:

> In its desire to reconcile man with nature, save him from a lingering death and physical decrepitude and safeguard his primitive virtues and his natural environment, fascism was possibly the first environmentalist ideology of this century, combining the pursuit of technical progress and industrial growth with the protection of nature as the environment in which a civilization of leisure and sport could flourish.[49]

The Nazis enacted significant conservation and wilderness-protection programs.[50] The emphasis on health and fitness was part of the Nazis' back-to-nature movement. Whereas the traditions of the Enlightenment sought to transcend nature, fascist ideology made nature central to human life. In the words of Adolf Hitler, "the folkish philosophy of life corresponds to the innermost will of Nature."[51]

That the Nazis were the century's first environmentalists should by no means discredit the legitimate goals of today's environmental movement. Still, the exaltation of natural values can conflict with human values. The position of the contemporary Finnish environmentalist and Green Party activist Pentti Linkola has been called "Eco-Fascism."[52] Linkola, surveying the way humanity has ravaged nature, considers human beings to be an evolutionary mistake, a cancer of the earth. He says that he has more sympathy for threatened insect species than for children dying of hunger in Biafra. Linkola rejects democracy, humanism, and nonviolence in favor of an authoritarian agrarian society. He favors compulsory sterilization and violent eco-terrorism. Concerned about overpopulation, Linkola believes that sacrificing billions might possibly save a million. He offers a parable to justify his openness to the extermination of human beings: A ship of 100 passengers capsizes. Only one lifeboat is launched with room for 10. Those who hate life will try to rescue all of the passengers, loading the boat with more and more people until it sinks and everyone drowns. Those who love life, on the other hand, "will take the ship's axe and sever the hands that cling to the sides of the boat."[53]

What energized the fascist ideology, with its exaltation of culture and nature, was its revolutionary spirit and iconoclastic idealism. According to Sternhell, national socialists were taught "to despise anything that smacked of bourgeois or liberal values, to hold in contempt bourgeois virtues and morals, and the bourgeois' respect for the law, for legal forms, for democratic government."[54] Thus, fascism attracted students, artists, intellectuals, and the avant-garde. Fascists sought first of all to demolish Western civilization, so that it could be replaced with a new organic, holistic culture.

Martin Heidegger was appointed rector of the University of Freiburg to preside over the Nazification of the university. In his "Rectoral Address," he foresees the possibility of a time "when the spiritual strength of the West fails and its joints crack, when this moribund semblance of a culture caves in and drags all forces into confusion and lets them suffocate in madness."[55] Such a collapse of the West can lead to the emergence of a new order. As Heidegger elsewhere says, "Precisely because we dare to assume the arduous task of demolishing a world that has grown old and rebuilding it in a truly new—that is, historical—way, we must be aware of the tradition."[56]

Heidegger's attack on the West is repeated over and over again by his followers today, who perhaps do not realize its original Nazi context. Heidegger opposed democracy and continued to do so even after the collapse of the Third Reich. Heidegger was also an important environmental theorist, whose critique of technology—though rooted in National Socialist organicism—has been enormously influential.[57]

Hirsch summarizes the postmodernists' rebellion against Western civilization and the traditions of liberal democracy. He goes on to make the connection between contemporary thought and that of the fascists and to warn of the implications:

> In mounting their attack on humanism, which they take to be the evil heart of Western culture, the postmodernists unavoidably, and perhaps unintentionally, align themselves with the languages and agendas of the most destructive ideologies of our time [i.e., Marxism and fascism]. If it is true that "humanism" has not lived up to its promise of freedom, equality, and justice for all human beings, then an antihumanism that arises out of intellectual movements that resulted in such massive destruction of both the concept and the reality of human dignity (whether in the gulag or the KZ-Lager) hardly seems to be an appropriate antidote. It was, after all, the Nazi attack on humanism and its destruction of the ideal of human dignity that fueled the most bestial cruelties of the SS.[58]

The fascists did not shrink from the implications of their ideas. Their advocacy of totalitarianism meant the integration of all of life into a total organic unity. The state—that is, the social organization conceived as the embodiment of the culture—becomes everything. As Mussolini said, "We control political forces, we control moral forces, we control economic forces." Anticipating the Nazi eugenics programs, Mussolini said that the state "necessarily transforms people even in their physical aspect."[59] The state would be transformed into a living organism, in which each individual would find fulfillment and purpose, like cells in a greater body.

Adolf Hitler summed up his goal of replacing a lifeless, alienating Western civilization with a new organic society:

> With the founding of the NSDAP [the Nazi party], for the first time

41

a movement had appeared whose goal did not, like that of the bourgeois parties, consist in a mechanical restoration of the past, but in the effort to erect an organic folkish state in place of the present senseless state mechanism.[60]

His goal was not at all reactionary, in the sense of a "conservative" return to the past. Rather, Hitler was attempting to create something new, to replace a lifeless "mechanism" with an "organic folkish state," that is, a unified society fully integrated with culture and with nature.

Hitler did not come to power by promoting terror, world war, and holocaust. These were the *effects* of his ideas. Although Hitler never hid the dark side of his ideology,[61] his promotion of cultural identity, environmentalism, and economic justice were very persuasive. His populist politics and his avant-garde philosophy made him popular with both the masses and the intellectual elite. The problem was that so few people understood where these ideas would lead—that his economic program would lead to slavery; that the privileging of the culture over the individual would mean the erasure of human freedom and dignity; that the glorification of nature would result in antihuman brutality; that the impulse to be primitive would result in barbarism; that his rejection of traditional morality would result in mass murder.

3

"The Hebrew Disease" Fascist Theology

Christianity, sprung from Jewish roots and comprehensible only as a growth on this soil, represents the counter-movement to any morality of breeding, of race, of privilege: it is the anti-Aryan religion par excellence.

—Nietzsche[1]

First the invisible but all-seeing, the unattainable but all-demanding God of Sinai. Second the terrible sweetness of Christ. Had the Jew not done enough to sicken man? . . . Look at them: prophets, martyrs, smashers of images, word spinners drunk with the terror of the absolute. It was only a step, gentlemen, a small, inevitable step, from Sinai to Nazareth, from Nazareth to the covenant of Marxism. . . . The Jew has pressed on us the blackmail of transcendence.

—George Steiner's fictional portrayal of Hitler
in *The Portage to San Cristbal of A. H.* (1981)[2]

Fascism cannot be understood except in terms of its self-proclaimed opposite, its archnemesis—the Jew. The heart of Nazism, as Hannah Arendt has observed, is anti-Jewishness.[3] The Nazi hatred of the Jews was more than racial. To be sure, the racial biologists considered the Jews to be an inferior race. The fascist ideal of cultural identity also excluded the Jews, as ethnic outsiders, from participation in the larger society. National Socialist economy theory blamed the Jews for "banking capitalism." The Nazis skillfully played on centuries of anti-Semitism among the ordinary people. But the enmity between the Nazis and the Jews went even deeper.

Fascists hated the Jews not merely because of their race but because of their ideas and their worldview. They sought to exterminate the Jews; they also sought to exterminate the Jewish influence in Western culture. The Hebraic heritage was mediated in the West by the Bible. Christianity too was to be purged of its Jewish elements, that is, its Biblicism.

Anti-Hebraism

Fascism has been defined as "the practical and violent resistance to transcendence."[4] Fascist spirituality is one of immanence. A mysticism of nature and community, the land and the blood, would heal the alienation of modern life. The Jews, on the other hand, were the source of transcendent religion, with all of its implications.

A common motif of Nazi anti-Semitism was that Jews were cerebral and abstract, detached from life and from nature. This is Paul De Man's point in one of the anti-Semitic essays he wrote for a collaborationist periodical: "Their cerebralness, their capacity to assimilate doctrines while maintaining a cold detachment from them" is one of "the specific characteristics of the Jewish mind."[5] Such a way of thinking is intrinsically alienating, and the Nazis considered alienation to be the specific legacy of the Jews.

The foundation of the Hebrew tradition is monotheism. It was a common complaint of fascist intellectuals that the Jews invented the idea of the one God. According to the poet and fascist propagandist Ezra Pound, the Jewish religion began when Moses, "having to keep a troublesome rabble in order" scared them by inventing "a disagreeable bogie, which he ... [called] a god."[6] Since then, concludes Pound, "The greatest tyrannies have arisen from the dogma that the *theos* is one, or that there is a unity above the various strata of theos which imposes its will upon the substrata, and thence upon human individuals."[7]

By asserting the existence of only one transcendent God, so the argument goes, the Jews drained the immanent world of its spiritual significance. The rich polytheism of the ancient pagan world, in which nature was permeated by spiritual beings, was banished. Jewish monotheism led to the decline of mythological consciousness, in which religion, nature, and the community were unified.[8] Fascism sought to restore the values of primitive cultures, with their social solidarity, oneness with nature, and psychic integration. The iconoclasm, antipaganism, and moralism of the Judeo-Christian tradition must be eradicated so that a more holistic spirituality could emerge. The fascists sought to remythologize modern life.

Monotheism exorcised the gods from nature, leaving behind a natural order that is empty and mechanical. Nature, no longer seen as sacred, thus became vulnerable to scientific exploitation. Human beings became cut off from nature, alienated from the natural order. This fascist and anti-Semitic brand of environmentalism is exemplified in the writings of the French proto-fascist Charles Maurras. His ideal was to achieve an organic unity of life. Modern economics, technology, and science, according to Maurras, are "anti-nature." All are encouraged by monotheism and fostered by the Jew.[9]

That Jews are antinature became a constant refrain of Nazi anti-Semitism.[10] This charge against the Jews and the alternative project of reprivileging nature is a major theme of *Mein Kampf*. Thus, Hitler derides the notion that " 'Man's role is to overcome Nature!' Millions thoughtlessly parrot this Jewish nonsense.... Man has never yet conquered nature in anything."[11] His new order will bring natural principles back into human life.

Hebraic monotheism has ethical implications, which the fascists found particularly abhorrent. The One God is righteous, and the source of transcendent moral law. Right and wrong are not determined by nature, nor by the community, nor by human choice. Rather, God reveals absolute moral principles, which transcend nature, the community, and the self, all of which come under God's judgment.

Robert Casillo summarizes Pound's attack on the ethical heritage of monotheism:

> [For Pound] another pernicious instrument of monotheistic tyranny is ethical absolutism or "code-worship" .... Unlike the flexible Greeks, [the Jews] follow rigid laws and formal procedures and a categorical set of moral standards (the Ten Commandments) which now have a wide if not universal application.... As monotheism severs man from Nature, so its categorical morality alienates man from his natural impulses. This is why Pound considers Judaism the religion *par excellence* of punishment and repression, of the "forbidden," of "taboo." Repeatedly he emphasizes the "brute disorder" of Jewish taboos and the Jews' responsibility for the "sadistic and masochistic tendencies" of Christianity.[12]

The fascists preferred a relativized ethic based upon the claims of nature, the needs of the community, and the assertion of the human will. Such an ethic could override the categorical "Thou shalt not kill." The Holocaust could thus be permitted.

Monotheism furthermore worked against the idea that truth and moral values are relative. Pound complained that whereas polytheistic cultures were pluralistic, monotheism asserted one "universal truth" for everyone.[13] He blamed Jewish monotheism for the West's "intolerance, monopoly, and uniformity."[14]

The irony of a fascist attacking intolerance becomes most grotesque in *Mein Kampf*. Hitler has been arguing that opposing positions must not be tolerated; he then backpedals, remembering the notion that intolerance comes from the Jews:

> The objection may very well be raised that such phenomena in world history [the necessity of intolerance] arise for the most part from specifically Jewish modes of thought, in fact, that this type of intolerance and fanaticism positively embodies the Jewish nature. This may be a thousand times true; we may deeply regret this fact and establish with justifiable loathing that its appearance in the history of mankind is something that was previously alien to history—yet this does not alter the fact that this condition *is* with us today.[15]

In other words, the Jews with their absolute morality invented intolerance; therefore, they shall not be tolerated.

The Hebraic and Biblical ethic had profound political implications. There is a higher law than that of the state. Nations, no less than individuals, are subject to those objective moral absolutes whose authority is grounded in the transcendent God. Morality is not cultural, but theological. Because of these transcendent moral standards, it is possible to criticize the state and its leaders.[16]

For mythological cultures, such as the Canaanites, the king was semidivine. The social order was understood to be one with the religious and natural order. Thus, social laws, customs, and the dictates of those in power were fully sanctioned by the mythological worldview. It was thus literally unthinkable to criticize the king, since there was no conceptual framework for asserting any higher authority. Social change, in the direction of greater mercy or justice, was practically unheard of. Even customs horrific to the Judeo-Christian mind such as child sacrifice were accepted even by the parents of the victim. This is how the crops grow. The gods, the king, the spirits of nature, the needs of the community, and reality itself require that the child be given to Moloch.

The Hebrew prophets, on the other hand, excoriated kings and whole cultures for the evil they were committing. They demanded that those in power change their ways and change their societies according to the objective righteousness of God. Jeremiah was a social critic:

> This is what the LORD says: "Go down to the palace of the king of Judah and proclaim this message there: 'Hear the word of the LORD, O king of Judah, you who sit on David's throne—you, your officials and your people who come through these gates. This is what the LORD says: Do what is just and right. Rescue from the hand of his oppressor the one who has been robbed. Do no wrong or violence to the alien, the fatherless or the widow, and do not shed innocent blood in this place. For if you are careful to carry out these commands, then kings who sit on David's throne will come through the gates of this palace, riding in chariots and on horses, accompanied by their officials and their people. But if you do not obey these commands, declares the LORD, I swear by myself that this palace will become a ruin.' " (Jeremiah 22:1–5)

That a prophet could come into the presence of a king and denounce him for oppression and bloodshed on the higher authority of the "word of God" was a conceptual development of the profoundest importance for Western society. We are so used to criticizing our leaders and our society that we take it for granted, but this is only because the Judeo-Christian ethic is so deeply grounded in Western thought, which ever since has had a tradition of social criticism and moral reform.

Nothing, however, could be more radically disruptive to the organic social order of the ancient Canaanites or to the communalism advocated by the fascists. Such an ethic alienated individuals from their communities. It created discontent and disunity. Devotion is turned away from one's community and one's homeland to a God who insists that the community and homeland must be changed. The result is instability, constant social change, and, as always, alienation.

Charles Maurras indicts the Jews, and with them the whole Biblical tradition, for these very reasons. "The Jew, a monotheist and fed by the prophets, has become an agent of the revolution."[17] Repeating the charge that monotheism is "anti-nature," Maurras attacks "prophetism" for undermining the organic social order. He goes on to attack monotheism for promoting the concept of individual liberty.[18] Robert Casillo summarizes his argument:

> As Maurras recognized, monotheism, by asserting a transcendental absolute for all men, tends to destroy society's "beautiful" and natural "inequalities." Even where social inequalities exist, monotheism democratizes the realm of the spirit and thus lessens differences between men. This is why Maurras finds in Jewish monotheism the ultimate enemy of hierarchy and the ultimate source of liberalism.[19]

Casillo, answering Pound's charge of Jewish intolerance, counters that "monotheism is largely anti-exploitive, implying that the same spiritual truth and salvation is available for all."[20]

Another fascist thinker, Leòn van Huffel, in an article accompanying one of Paul De Man's, argues against a merely "social" anti-Semitism in favor of a "scientific" anti-Semitism. Van Huffel, as Alice Yaeger Kaplan summarizes his essay, argues that man doesn't live for

> abstractions such as liberty, equality and fraternity but that he carries in his blood the concrete mark of previous generations. Liberal, individualist and atomistic philosophies must be countered with a "collective and organic conception of societies."[21]

Van Huffel blames the Jewish prophetic tradition for secular manifestations such as the French revolution and liberal democracy. The Jews are responsible for "individualist and atomistic" political philosophies, which must be replaced with those that are "collective and organic."

Transcendent, and thus Hebraic, moral abstractions such as liberty, equality, and fraternity must be given up to achieve a "collective and organic" society. In such a society, the individual becomes one with the group. Hierarchy is a necessity. In nature the strong have prerogatives over the weak, and in natural collectives—in a beehive, a flock of birds, or a wolf pack—there is a pecking order and hierarchical roles so that the whole group can survive. In nature, there is no equality, nor is there liberty. Animals obey their instincts; their actions are determined by nature and by the needs of their species.

Culturally, equality and liberty are also illusions. Everyone has cultural roles, which tend to involve social hierarchies. Culture—not individual choices and rational decision-making—is actually what shapes the individual personality. There is no personal identity apart from cultural identity. A "collective and organic" society must be based on different principles than the "individualist and atomistic" ideals injected into Western culture by the Jews.

For those who reject transcendent moral absolutes—such as "Thou shalt not kill"—there was nothing to prevent the gas chambers. There was no higher authority than the "collective and organic" society, which sought to rid itself both of the Jewish people and of their ideas.

Anti-Christianity

Christianity, insofar as it is based on the Bible, is also intrinsically Hebraic, and it too was the object of fascist contempt. Hitler insisted that Christianity was the severest blow mankind had suffered. St. Paul was a bolshevik. Christianity allowed slaves to revolt against their masters. Christianity destroyed Rome. And it was all an invention of the Jew.[22]

"With the appearance of Christianity," wrote Hitler, "the first spiritual terror entered into the far freer ancient world."[23] The terrorist and quencher of freedom Adolf Hitler here condemns Christianity for terrorizing people spiritually and restricting pagan freedom. Such ghastly irony is one of the implications of the fascist assault upon Judeo-Christian objective morality.

According to fascist theorists, objective moral laws create guilt and restrict the natural passions. Ezra Pound blames "the Hebrew disease" for "asceticisms," "belief that the body is evil," and every feature of Christianity that is "anti-life" and "anti-flesh."[24]

Hitler and Pound make the fascist ethic seem permissive and hedonistic. In one sense it was, especially in its early phase, which was part of its attraction in Bohemian circles. Individual appetites, however, were subject to the needs of the "collective and organic" society. The fascists talk about moral freedom, but they reject political freedom. While they assail the Judeo-Christian tradition for its intolerance and fostering of guilt, they also assail it for its altruism, for protecting the weak against the strong, and for its implications of equality and political liberty. Ezra Pound complained that there was no "sense of social order in the teachings of the irresponsible protagonist of the New Testament."[25]

If Judeo-Christian transcendent ethics place restrictions on individual behavior, they also liberate the individual socially and politically. The fascists' ethics of immanence did the reverse—they unleashed the animal impulses, while enslaving the population.

Christianity, complained Pound, "is riddled with semitism."[26] A theme of *Mein Kampf* is the conflict between "nature" and "anti-nature." For Hitler, both Judaism and Christianity are "anti-nature."[27] That is, they are transcendent. Hitler's project of forging a counter-spirituality that would find fulfillment in the immanent realm meant that Christianity, no less than Judaism, would be his enemy.

Whereas Hitler could deal with the Jews by a policy of extermination, Christianity could not be dealt with so neatly. Christianity, after all, had become part of the texture of the ethnic culture that he was trying to restore. If Christianity could not be eliminated, it could be changed. Cured of its "Hebrew disease," Christianity could be repaganized.

Hitler hated Christianity, but expressed a perverse admiration for Catholicism.[28] Ezra Pound and Charles Maurras repeat the paradox. According to Ernst Nolte,

> Maurras has made little effort to hide the fact that he really wants to attack Christ and regards Catholicism as un-Christian precisely because, to him, Catholicism is the incomparable masterpiece of pagan and secular wisdom which by a hierarchical system of mediators makes the church the spokesman of man and eliminates both Father and Son.[29]

Catholicism makes the transcendent immanent. It does so by bringing the spiritual down to earth by tangible means in a collective, hierarchical, and authoritarian institution. Pound liked Catholicism for its pagan roots.[30] The cults of the saints are close to the old polytheism. The liturgical calendar aligns human beings with the cycles of nature. Catholic rituals are communal, binding individuals together into a "collective and organic" culture.

In the Middle Ages, the sacred and the secular were integrated; society was unified in a hierarchical order in which everyone knew his or her place; the alienations and uncertainties of the modern world did not exist. Fascism was thus able to draw on the medievalism that was a legacy of the late romantics.

The fact is, orthodox Christianity has always affirmed *both* the transcendence of God *and* His immanence. God is omnipresent. He has become incarnate in Jesus Christ. He is present in the sacraments. Ordinary human life is charged with significance. Judaism too stresses the historicity of God's actions and the importance of daily obedience in the mundane details of life. At the same time, God is beyond and above the universe. While God's glory did fill the temple, Solomon realizes that "the heavens, even the highest heaven, cannot contain you. How much less this temple I have built!" (1 Kings 8:27). The problem is not alienation from nature, but alienation from God through the rebellion of sin. This alienation can be healed by God's grace and redemption. To deny half of the paradox—whether between transcendence and immanence, or Christ's divinity and humanity—is to fall into heresy.

While it is true that Catholic nationalists often turned to fascism, it is also true that ultimately Catholicism and fascism clashed. According to Victor Farias, Martin Heidegger was once a devout Catholic, under the tutelage of Father Engelbert Krebs. A number of proto-fascist groups attempted to combine Catholicism with an extreme nationalism and anti-Semitism. Farias suggests that the influence of these extremist groups eventually led Heidegger to National Socialism.[31]

Later, however, Heidegger formally abandoned his earlier faith, which conflicted with both his philosophical and political program. As Hirsch observes, "Heidegger, like the Nazi ideologues, wanted to break with Hebraism, as well as 'metaphysics.' But to achieve such a rupture, Christian and humanist values would have to be discarded too."[32] Heidegger became overtly hostile to Christianity. Farias cites his "virulent anti-Catholicism" and his frustrated efforts as rector of the University of Marburg to suppress Catholicism among his students.[33]

Heidegger, far from being merely a fellow traveler, actually became a member of the most radical Nazi faction. Although most of the Catholic students tended to support National Socialism, Heidegger insisted on persecuting them for their Catholicism. Heidegger's heavy-handed attempts to suppress Catholic student groups proved too extreme even for Hitler's regime, which wanted to keep

Catholic support. When Heidegger's political patrons were purged from the Nazi party—incredible as it may seem—for being too extreme, he lost his rectorate.[34]

Fascists assumed that there could be a Catholicism without Christianity. Of course, they were wrong. The symptoms of the "Hebrew disease" kept manifesting themselves. Heidegger must have been especially irritated by his old spiritual advisor Father Krebs. While Heidegger was becoming a famous philosopher by trying to purge Western thought of Hebraism, Father Krebs was speaking out against anti-Semitism. Acting in the tradition of the Biblical prophets by speaking out against objective evil, Father Krebs became a leader in the Catholic resistance movement.[35]

If the fascist theorists were able to accommodate a paganized Catholicism, Protestantism was anathema. For Ezra Pound, Protestantism is only Judaism in disguise.[36] Pound blamed the Reformation for the revival of Hebrew texts and ways of thinking, and thus for the decline of Europe.[37] That is to say, the Reformation reintroduced the Bible into Western culture.

Protestantism, according to Maurras, released the "poison" of monotheism.[38] Maurras attacks Protestantism because it is Jewish.[39] He writes,

> The fathers of the [democratic] revolution are in Geneva, in Wittenberg, and in more ancient times in Jerusalem; they derive from the Jewish spirit and from varieties of an independent Christianity which were rampant in Eastern deserts and Teutonic forests, in the various focal points of barbarism.[40]

Such tirades against the Reformation assume the same tone and the same rhetoric as Maurras's anti-Semitic invective.

As is often the case, the fascist intellectuals are right in their analysis, although they condemn what others would praise. Paul Gottfried, in reviewing Farias's book on Heidegger, agrees that "German Catholicism and its explicitly medieval heritage was more open to anti-Semitism than German Protestantism." He concludes that "despite Luther's anti-Jewish outbursts, the Reformation he launched gave new emphasis to Christianity's Hebraic roots for the first time since the primitive Church."[41]

Biblical Protestantism was as irreconcilable to fascism as Judaism. And yet Protestantism too was deeply ingrained in European and especially German culture. If the fascists thought they could appropriate Catholicism, they had to take a different approach with Protestantism. Taking advantage of the lax doctrinal structure of the official Protestant church, the fascists simply had to change its theology. If they could excise the authority of the Bible, the heart of Protestantism would be cut out. The fascist theologians could use the institutional shell that remained as a framework for the new "folkish" faith.

The attack on the Bible within Protestantism was the work of both textual scholars and theologians. By the 20th century, the "higher criticism" of the Old Testament, which undercut traditional ideas about the authorship and composition of the Bible, had already weakened the doctrine of Biblical authority. By assuming that the Biblical text and the events it describes are to be explained in naturalistic, scientific terms, historical-critical scholarship vitiated the Bible's status as supernatural revelation.

Soon German scholars such as Friedrich Delitzsch were taking the next step. In 1902–1903, Delitzsch, a Biblical scholar from the University of Berlin, published a book arguing that the Old Testament was dependent upon Babylonian culture and mythology.[42] His position was controversial, but it represents a fairly typical example of modern Biblical criticism. Delitzsch's scholarship led him to conclude in a later work that

> the Old Testament was full of deceptions of all kinds—a veritable hodge-podge of erroneous, incredible, undependable figures, including those of Biblical chronology; a veritable labyrinth of betrayals, of misleading reworkings, revisions, and transpositions, and, therefore, of anachronisms; a constant inter-mixture of contradictory particulars and whole stories, unhistorical inventions, legends, folk-tales—in short, a book full of intentional and unintentional deceptions (in part, self-deceptions), a very dangerous book in the use of which the greatest care is necessary.[43]

It soon becomes clear, however, that the reason Delitzsch believes the Old Testament is "a very dangerous book" is because it is Jewish.

Delitzsch goes so far as to argue that Jesus was not Jewish. Following the party line of other anti-Semites, Delitzsch distinguishes between Jews and Galileans, who came from northern bloodlines. As further evidence, he cites the difference between

Jesus, with his warm humanitarianism, and the Jewish mind, with its moral intolerance. "Delitzsch could find no bridge between the Old Testament and Jesus' mentality" and "contended that Christianity is an absolutely new religion, totally distinct from that of the Old Testament."[44]

The Old Testament therefore, he argued, should have no place in the education of Protestant pastors. Although it might still be taught in an Oriental studies department or as part of the history of religion, the Old Testament should be banished from the schools of theology. As Raymond Surburg summarizes the Delitsch position,

> The New Testament should be studied without consulting the Old Testament, and teachers should teach New Testament courses in such a way as to show students the errors of Jewish evangelists who found Christ foretold in the Old Testament. Delitzsch argued for freeing the New Testament from the embrace of the Old Testament and further recommended that Jesus' teaching should be reduced to its original purity for the blessing of the Christian church.[45]

Of course, such "reducing" of the New Testament by purging it of the Old would also be done by the historical-critical approach to Scripture. With the New Testament truncated and de-Hebraized, the Word of God could be fully subjugated to an anti-Semitic ideology.

Delitzsch was by no means a mere Nazi propagandist or a crackpot. He is considered the founder of Assyriology, he was a distinguished scholar of his time, and his work for the most part is still respected by Biblical critics.[46] His complete rejection of the Old Testament was not uncommon. Adolf von Harnack, the influential liberal theologian, also believed that Christianity was completely distinct from Judaism and that the Old Testament should be taken out of the Bible.[47]

What is left when the Bible is taken out of Protestantism? There are two possibilities, both of which have been developed by 20th-century theologians and both of which came together in the fascist church.

Christianity could be transformed into a cultural religion. Instead of attending to otherworldly concepts such as individual salvation and everlasting life, the church would focus upon this world. Moral pronouncements, social involvement, and political activism would become *the* work of the church. Such "cultural Protestant-ism," to use H. Richard Niebuhr's term, came to dominate 19th-century Protestantism and continued as a major strain of 20th-century theology.[48]

For all of its apparent "liberalism," *cultural* Protestantism, like fascism, rejects the transcendent in favor of a religion centered wholly upon the immanent world. Those who believed that "the world sets the agenda for the church," to use a modern slogan of liberal theology, were easily manipulated by fascist ideology. They lacked a transcendent reference point from which they could criticize the existing society. Their impulse to help the society became directed by the Nazis' diagnosis of the society's ills.

To be sure, many liberals opposed the Nazis—often in the name of another secular ideology such as Marxism rather than on Biblical grounds. But, as Robert Ericksen has observed, "many of the most enthusiastic supporters of Nazism among theologians were in the nineteenth-century liberal theological tradition."[49]

Even Hitler praised "positive Christianity," by which he meant a focus on the life of Jesus. He only opposed "negative Christianity," the focus on Christ's death and sacrifice, which he, like liberals from the time of Matthew Arnold, attributed to the malign influence of St. Paul.[50] Christianity drained of the supernatural was no competitor to the Nazi mysticism of the blood and the soil. Indeed, if Christianity could be reduced to a vague ethical idealism, it could serve the state by encouraging self-sacrifice and social solidarity.

Better yet, the new fascist spirituality could be injected into the church, filling the spiritual void left by rationalistic liberalism, while transforming the church into a vehicle for the new ideology. This was the project of the "German Christian" movement, which, with Hitler's accession, gained control of the institutional church in Germany. Christianity could be reinvented, that is to say, repaganized; it only had to be drained of its Biblical and Hebraic content.

4

"Two Masters" Fascism vs. Confessionalism

If there is one clear portal to the 20th century, it is a passage through the death of God, the collapse of any meaning or reality lying beyond the newly discovered radical immanence of modern man, an immanence dissolving even the memory of the shadow of transcendence.

—Thomas Altizer, *Gospel of Christian Atheism* (1967)[1]

Verily a man cannot serve two masters. And I consider the foundation or destruction of a religion far greater than the foundation or destruction of a state.

—Adolf Hitler, *Mein Kampf* (1927)[2]

The ultimate goal of the Nazis was to eliminate not only the Jews but the Judeo-Christian tradition, with its transcendent God and transcendent ethics. They sought to replace it with either a paganized Christianity or a revival of ancient mythological consciousness. To this end, the *German Christian* movement took shape. Making use of the current theological scholarship and placing itself in the mainstream of modern theology, the *German Christian* movement sought to synthesize fascism and Christianity.

In doing so, however, they sparked a reaction of *Confessional Christianity*. The enormities of fascism led many Christians to rediscover the historic Christian confessions and the authority of the Hebraic scriptures. Their commitment to this transcendent faith led them to resistance and, in many cases, arrest and martyrdom.

The "Church Struggle" between the syncretists and the confessionalists during the Nazi regime was a pivotal and defining moment for the Christian faith in the modern era. Should Christianity be redefined along the lines of prevailing intellectual and cultural trends? Or should it maintain its commitment to transcendent doctrines and transcendent ethics as mediated in the Hebraic scriptures? Nazism forced theologians, pastors, and laypeople to choose which model of Christianity they would follow. Those who agreed to syncretism could enjoy power and influence. Those who held to confessionalism and its implications faced arrest by the Gestapo.

In religious circles today, the conflict between syncretism and confessionalism continues. The assault on Hebraism is continuing in mainline theology and in the culture as a whole. The Biblical heritage is being critiqued in the very same terms used by the early fascists. The politicized, this-worldly Christianity of much contemporary theology and the New Age neopaganism of the popular culture have close parallels to fascist spirituality. The *Church Struggle* is far from over.

The "German Christians"

The *German Christian* movement, as described by a church historian, "articulated a highly politicized and secularized theology that subverted scripture and the inherited Lutheran and Reformed confessions with führer-worship, German völkischness, and explicitly racial anti-Semitism."[3] Theologians, church officials, and pastors were its theorists and its leaders. The movement was not a conspiracy by the Nazi party, but a genuine theological movement within the church.

The state Protestant church, known as *the German Evangelical Church,* was an amalgam of Lutheran, Reformed, and United congregations. They all received "church taxes" as collected by the state and were united in an official bureaucratic structure. Once Hitler was in power, the *German Christians* took control of the machinery of the state church.

Hitler had negotiated a *concordat* with the Vatican, which, despite its compromises limiting the political involvement of the church and its ability to defend the Jews, did limit Nazi interference in the Catholic Church.[4] The free churches—those Protestant bodies such as the Free Lutherans and Methodists who refused membership in the state church—were also relatively free from overt Nazi control. The uneasy truce between the Catholic and the Free churches and the Nazi party did not, of course, exempt these churches from the moral and spiritual pressures of the times. In time, the party violated the Concordat and Catholics faced overt persecution. Still, the formal separation between church and state at least gave these churches some breathing room. The *German Christians,* however, in gaining control of the major Protestant religious institution, could proceed with the Nazification of the church.

What this meant can be seen in a research institute established by the new church government: *The Institute for the Study of Jewish Influence on German Church Life.* One of its scholars, Dr. Ernst Bergmann, gave lectures on "The De-Judaization of Religious Life as the Task of German Theology and Church" and wrote books arguing that Jesus was not a Jew. The institute sponsored research on "The Influence of Judaism on Catholicism from the Blood-Racial and Spiritual-Religious Point of View."[5] A revised version of the New Testament was published which omitted such "Jewish" terms as *Jehovah, Israel, Zion,* and *Jerusalem.*[6]

In November, 1933, a mass *German Christian* rally was held in a sports stadium in Berlin. Resolutions were passed attacking the Jewish influence on Christianity. One resolution demanded the purging of all pastors who rejected "the spirit of National Socialism." It insisted that the "Aryan paragraph," the policy of excluding all people of Jewish descent from office, be applied within the church. Pastors with Jewish ancestry, as well as baptized Jewish converts, were to be expelled from the ministry. Another resolution actually called for the removal of the Old Testament from the Bible.[7] The conference categorically rejected the very foundations of Judeo-Christian transcendent morality:

> We expect that our nation's church as a German People's Church should free itself from all things not German in its services and confession, especially from the Old Testament with its Jewish system of quid pro quo morality.[8]

No Christian who had even a vestige of belief in the authority of Scripture could stomach such flagrant heresies.

The rally caused an uproar throughout the German church. Christians were forced to take stock of their beliefs and the foundations for those beliefs. The controversy sparked by this rally precipitated an organized counter-movement of *Confessional Christianity*.

The Confessing Church

The *Confessing Church* was organized to combat the *German Christian* movement. The name *Confessing* alluded to the *Confessions* of the church, the historical Christian doctrines collected, for example, in the Lutheran *Book of Concord*. Whether they had been conservative, liberal, or followers of the new dialectical theology, the Christians who opposed Hitler and the fascist worldview did so by reemphasizing the classical doctrines of the church. "In this struggle under the attacks of 'German Christian' doctrines," writes one scholar, "they experienced an amazing rediscovery of the Reformation Confessions. And in this act of confession an unexpected partnership with the so-called former liberals and orthodox positivists emerged."[9] The Confessing Christians were those who held to a doctrinal, transcendent, and thus for the Nazis a "Jewish," Christianity against the syncretic, this-worldly, and paganized religion of the *German Christians*.

To clearly address the doctrinal issues, the *Confessing Church* drew up a Confession of its own, the Barmen Declaration. In the words of its prologue, "the Confessional Synod calls upon the congregations to range themselves behind it in prayer, and steadfastly to gather around those pastors and teachers who are loyal to the Confessions."[10] They were to do so on the basis of the transcendently authoritative Word of God: "If you find that we are speaking contrary to Scripture, then do not listen to us! But if you find that we are taking our stand upon Scripture, then let no fear or temptation keep you from treading with us the path of faith and obedience to the Word of God."

The Barmen Declaration consisted of six articles. Because the authority of the Bible was one of the key issues, each article began with a quotation from Scripture. Following the form of the classic Lutheran confession, the *Formula of Concord*, each article then stated both theses and antitheses, affirmations of the *Confessional* doctrine and rejections of the contrary doctrines as taught by the *German Christians*.

The first article affirms that "Jesus Christ, as he is attested for us in Holy Scripture, is the one Word of God which we have to hear and which we have to trust and obey in life and in death." Thus, Christ is affirmed as the transcendent authority and source of values, as revealed in the language of the Bible. "We reject the false doctrine, as though the church could and would have to acknowledge as a source of its proclamation, apart from and besides this one Word of God, still other events and powers, figures and truths, as God's revelation."

Such a rejection is startling in the context of modern theology. Not only does it condemn the *German Christian* notion that God reveals Himself in history—i.e., in the German race, the Nazi revolution, and the person of Adolf Hitler. It is a wholesale rejection of "natural theology" and its consequent syncretism. The assumption that God is revealed in nature and in human culture, that He is accessible by reason and by historical progress, had become almost a commonplace of modernist theology. Instead, as Arthur Cochrane has shown, the Barmen Declaration goes back to the Reformation Confessions of the 16th century to affirm that revelation is in Christ alone and Scripture alone.[11]

The broader scope of the Barmen Declaration's rejection of natural theology is made explicit in the commentary to the declaration by Hans Asmussen, which was also adopted by the Synod of Barmen:

> We are raising a protest against the same phenomenon that has been slowly preparing the way for the devastation of the Church for more than two hundred years. For it is only a relative difference whether, in the church along with Holy Scripture, historical events or reason, culture, aesthetic feelings, progress, or other powers and figures are said to be binding claims upon the Church.[12]

The Barmen Declaration thus sets itself against not only the *German Christian* aberration but against the whole tradition of modernist syncretism that made it possible.

The other articles of the Declaration develop this theme with boldness and precision. Article 2 asserts the sovereignty of Christ over all of life. Article 3 asserts Christ's lordship over the church and rejects "the false doctrine, as though the Church were permitted to abandon the form of its message and order to its own pleasure or to changes in prevailing ideological and political conventions."

This is to say, the world does *not* set the agenda for the church. Article 4 teaches that church offices are for mutual service and ministry, not for the exercise of raw power. Article 5 acknowledges the divine appointment of the state, but rejects the pretensions of the state to "become the single and totalitarian order of human life, thus fulfilling the Church's vocation as well." Article 6 affirms the church's commission to proclaim the free grace of God to everyone by means of the Word and the sacraments. "We reject the false doctrine, as though the Church in human arrogance could place the Word and work of the Lord in the service of any arbitrarily chosen desires, purposes, and plans."

It may be true, as Robert Ericksen has suggested, that there was in the German church no clear "Hitler-proof" theology. Conservatives, liberals, and advocates of the new quasi-existentialist dialectical theology can all be found in both the pro-Hitler party and the *Confessional Church*.[13] And yet, in deciding whether or not to sign the Barmen Declaration and to participate in the shadow institution established by the *Confessing Synod*, the dividing line was clear. The *German Christians* clearly and explicitly rejected the Biblical revelation. Those who opposed them were drawn closer and closer to a reliance upon the Bible and the historic Christian Confessions. The Confessional movement allied dialectical theologians such as Barth and Bonhoeffer with orthodox Lutherans such as Hermann Sasse.[14]

The *German Christian* theologians predictably denounced the confessional movement as being "narrow" and "fundamentalist."[15] Cajus Fabricius marshalled 19th-century liberal scholarship with its focus upon an experiential and undogmatic religion to attack the Confessionalists.[16]

Perhaps the most formidable and sophisticated of the pro-Nazi theologians—and the most extreme in his commitment to fascism— was Emanuel Hirsch, a dialectical theologian. Considered "a major figure in twentieth-century German theology," Hirsch was "rooted in the existentialism that marked the best theologians of his generation."[17] Like other modernist theologians, Hirsch taught that the resurrection of Christ was only a spiritual vision. The Easter narratives were later additions to the New Testament. The idea of a physical resurrection distorts Christianity by focusing attention to the hereafter rather than to the present.[18] He criticized Christians who try to separate Christianity from culture.[19] He stressed the importance of community in the Christian life.[20]

Hirsch is thus clearly in the mainstream of modernist theology. A prominent Kierkegaard scholar, Hirsch became the Dean of the Theology faculty at Göttingen University. Ericksen finds many close affinities in his thought to the other great theologians of his day. Like his friend Paul Tillich, Hirsch articulated a Christian view of history that was both existential and political. (The main difference, according to Ericksen, is that Tillich's solution was a religious socialism of the left, while Hirsch advocated a Christian nationalism of the right.)[21] Like Rudolf Bultmann, he advocated demythologizing the New Testament. Like Dietrich Bonhoeffer, he advocated radical discipleship and the need to accept with honesty the task of bringing Christianity into the 20th century.[22]

Such major 20th-century theologians themselves had to decide where they stood in the conflict. Karl Barth, although a citizen of Switzerland, was a major founder of the Confessing movement and an author of the Barmen Declaration. His neoorthodox theology, with its emphasis on the transcendence of God and the revelation of the Word, set him clearly at odds with Nazi ideology. Another neoorthodox theologian, Dietrich Bonhoeffer, threw himself into the Confessional movement and the resistance against Hitler. His involvement in a plot to assassinate Hitler led to his arrest and execution.

The more liberal Paul Tillich left Germany, largely because of his Marxist brand of socialism. Rudolf Bultmann, who attempted to synthesize Heidegger and Christianity, laid low. He rejected the racial stance of the *German Christians* and is said to have signed the Barmen Declaration. But, as he admitted, "I have never directly and actively participated in political affairs."[23] He retained his professorship at Marburg University throughout the Nazi regime. Bultmann never opposed Hitler directly.

The political battles between the *Confessing Church* and the *German Christians* for control of the institutional church were complex. The *Confessing Church* set up a shadow government paralleling the institutional structure that was in the hands of the state apparatus. In some cases, whole sections of the institution remained under the control of the Confessionalists. Some congregations took a stand one way or another. Many congregations were split, with the two factions worshipping together, but in bitter enmity. Often the Confessionalists in a congregation met in small groups or Bible studies.[24] Statistics are uncertain, but records of the Pastor's Emergency League, a Confessional organization devoted to fighting the Aryan restrictions, list 4,952 members out of 18,184 active pastors.[25]

In this turmoil, it was also possible not to take a stand, itself a kind of commitment. Probably most pastors and church members steered away from the blatant heresies of the *German Christian* movement, while also staying away from the dangerous and seemingly unpatriotic efforts of the underground *Confessing Church.* Many sincerely believed in the National Socialist reforms and were able to keep their personal faith distinct from their political leanings.

This was no doubt bolstered by a misreading of Luther's "Two Kingdoms" approach to the relationship between church and state. According to this view, God rules the world in two distinct ways: His spiritual kingdom is in the church, whose rule is love and which administers forgiveness through the Gospel. God's earthly kingdom is maintained in the secular social order, whose rule is justice, administered by the Law. God is the ultimate authority behind earthly rulers, so that to disobey them is to disobey God. Critics have charged that this doctrine promoted passive obedience and unquestioning allegiance even to evil rulers such as Hitler. Actually, the doctrine of the two kingdoms insists that *God* is the king of both realms. An earthly ruler who breaks God's transcendent moral Law is usurping the divine authority. In the words of the Augsburg Confession, the central Lutheran doctrinal statement, "Christians are obliged to be subject to civil authority and obey its commands and laws in all that can be done without sin. But when commands of the civil authority cannot be obeyed without sin, we must obey God rather than men (Acts 5:29)."[26]

The case of the respected theologian Gerhard Kittel is probably representative of the confusion and vacillation within the German church. Kittel's religious conservatism kept him away from the *German Christians*; nevertheless, his political sympathies lay with the Nazis. At one point, Kittel argued that baptized Jews could be accepted as Christian brothers, but still persecuted as non-Germans![27]

Hitler himself in *Mein Kampf* summed up the ambivalence of German Protestantism, which tended to be patriotic, while having a core "Jewishness" that limited its usefulness to his cause:

Protestantism will always stand up for the advancement of all Germanism as such, as long as matters of inner purity or national deepening as well as German freedom are involved, since all these things have a firm foundation in its own being; but it combats with the greatest hostility any attempt to rescue the nation from the embrace of its most mortal enemy, since its attitude toward the Jews just happens to be more or less dogmatically established. Yet here we are facing the question without whose solution all other attempts at a German reawakening or resurrection are and remain absolutely senseless and impossible.[28]

The last sentence points ominously to the "final solution" to the problem of the Jews, with whom the Protestants are "dogmatically established."

Despite occasional inconsistencies and compromises, many Christians, both Catholic and Protestant, spoke out and acted boldly against the evils of the Nazi regime and faced martyrdom for their faith. When the euthanasia program began to be implemented in the hospitals, even many *German Christians* found themselves having to speak out against the regime.[29] The Confessional Bishop Theophil Wurm gave voice to the rumors of mass murders of Jews and forthrightly condemned Nazi genocide:

An end must also be made of all the measures through which members of other nations and races, without trial by civil or military courts, are put to death simply because they happen to belong to another nation or race. Such measures have become increasingly known through men on furlough, and they burden all Christian citizens because they contradict God's commandments just like the measures for elimination of the mentally sick, and they could cause terrible revenge on our people.[30]

Later, as the picture grew clearer, in statements that refute the notion that the German people knew nothing of the death camps, Bishop Wurm again spoke out:

I must, in agreement with the opinion of all positive Christian circles in Germany, declare that we Christians consider this extermination policy directed against the Jews as a great and disastrous injustice committed by Germany. Killing without justification because of war and without trial is against God's command, even if the government orders it, and as every deliberate violation of God's commandment is avenged, so will this be sooner or later.[31]

64

Bishop Wurm had already been arrested once by the Gestapo. Prayer lists circulating among the Confessional circles indicate that in 1937, more than 800 pastors were arrested.[32] The leader of the Confessing Church, Martin Niemöller, was sent to Dachau.[33] The Niemöller archives list over 125 pastors who were sent to concentration camps, to join thousands of clergymen from the occupied territories, including 2,579 priests in Dachau alone. 1,034 of them died in the camp.[34] Bonhoeffer's execution for his involvement in a plot to kill Hitler is well-known. His brother and two brothers-in-law were also killed. Many of his fellow conspirators, as well as others in the German resistance, were motivated by religious reasons.[35] The Niemöller archives mention 21 pastors who died for their faith, not counting those executed in the plot to kill Hitler.[36] While such numbers pale in magnitude before the slaughter of the Jews, at least some Christians were joining the Jews in a Biblical witness against fascism.

Nazi Spirituality

The true believers in National Socialism had no interest in the *German Christians'* project of reconciling fascist ideology with Christianity. For them, National Socialism was a religion in itself and should completely displace all other faiths.

Despite their fawning obsequiousness—or perhaps because of it—the *German Christians* were evidently held in contempt by the Nazi elite.[37] An internal note in the Propaganda Ministry responds to the "Institute for the Study of Jewish Influence on German Church Life," with its attempts to prove that Jesus was not Jewish and the like, with condescending dismissal: "The endeavors of this organization . . . are well meant, but there is no interest either in assimilating Christian teaching in national socialism or in proving that a re-shaped Christianity is not fundamentally Jewish."[38] Martin Bormann was more to the point:

National Socialist and Christian concepts cannot be reconciled. The Christian churches build on the ignorance of people and are anxious so far as possible to preserve this ignorance in as large a part of the populace as possible; only in this way can the Christian churches retain their power. In contrast, national socialism rests on scientific foundations.[39]

Hitler, of course, needed the support of the average German and was careful to keep up appearances. He kept statements such as Bormann's from circulating publicly and promoted a propaganda image of himself as a man who prayed and read the Bible.[40] Hitler maintained his membership in the Catholic Church and ordered top officials such as Göring and Goebbels, against their will, to stay on the rolls of their churches. To party insiders, he was more open, describing how "after difficult inner struggles I had freed myself of my remaining childhood religious conceptions. I feel as refreshed now as a foal on a meadow."[41] Hitler, having solved the "Jewish problem," planned to solve the "church problem" after the war:

> The war is going to be over. The last great task of our age will be to solve the church problem. It is only then that the nation will be wholly secure.... When I was young, my position was: Dynamite. It was only later that I understood that this sort of thing cannot be rushed. It must rot away like a gangrened member. The point that must be reached is to have the pulpits filled with none but boobs, and the congregations with none but little old women. The healthy young people are with us.[42]

While the leadership was ordered to stay on the church rolls for the time being, rank-and-file party members were encouraged to withdraw from their churches.[43] Members of the SS were forbidden to hold any leadership role in a church. Although they could retain formal membership, they were not allowed to worship in their uniforms, employ religious symbols, or sponsor lectures on religious topics. Hitler boasted that "I have six divisions of SS composed of men absolutely indifferent in matters of religion. It doesn't prevent them from going to their deaths with serenity in their souls."[44] As Himmler put it, "Men who can't divest themselves of manners of previous centuries, and scoff and sling mud at things which are holy and matters of belief to others, once and for all do not belong in the SS."[45]

As the Nazi party solidified its control and particularly with the outbreak of the war, the attempts to suppress and to replace the church became more overt. Church presses, including those that published the Bible, were shut down. Religious education was curtailed, and much church property was confiscated.[46] The Nazi party began scheduling its meetings and rallies—including compulsory

Hitler Youth gatherings—on Sunday mornings.[47] Not only was the party thus directly competing with church attendance, it was making itself a substitute for the church. Weddings and funeral services could be held apart from the church, using Nazi rituals. Efforts were made to substitute Hitler Youth dedication services for the rite of Confirmation.[48]

The Hitler Youth organization was a means of rebuilding society afresh by indoctrinating the next generation into the new order. One of the most dubious achievements of the *German Christians* was to merge the church's youth group, the Evangelical Youth Organization, with the Hitler Youth.[49] But even the staunchest *German Christian* parent must have been taken aback to hear camp songs such as this one:

> We are the happy Hitler Youth;
> We have no need of Christian virtue;
> For Adolf Hitler is our intercessor
> And our redeemer.
> No priest, no evil one
> Can keep us
> From feeling like Hitler's children.
> Not Christ do we follow, but Horst Wessel!
> Away with incense and holy water pots.
> Singing we follow Hitler's banners;
> Only then are we worthy of our ancestors.
> I am no Christian and no Catholic.
> I go with the SA through thick and thin.
> The Church can be stolen from me for all I care.
> The swastika makes me happy here on earth.
> Him will I follow in marching step;
> Baldur von Schirach, take me along.[50]

Even as Christianity is repudiated, its language—intercessor, redeemer—is appropriated and applied directly to Hitler.

The usurpation of the Judeo-Christian tradition by the new religion of National Socialism is perhaps most tellingly illustrated in a speech given to a student rally:

> I do not want to blaspheme God, but I ask: Who was greater, Christ or Hitler? Christ had at the time of his death twelve apostles, who, however, did not even remain true to him. Hitler, however,

today has a folk of 70 million behind him. We cannot tolerate that another organization is established alongside of us that has a different spirit than ours. We must crush it. National socialism in all earnestness says: I am the Lord thy God, thou shalt have no other gods before me.... Then ours is the kingdom and the power; for we have a strong Wehrmacht, and the glory—for we are again a respected nation, and may God will, in eternity. Heil Hitler![51]

Not only is Hitler said to be greater than Christ. National Socialism replaces monotheism, going so far as to assume the role of the one God of the Bible. With stunning blasphemy and idolatry, the Commandment to have no other gods is appropriated to enforce allegiance to the Nazi party. "National socialism in all earnestness says: I am the Lord thy God, thou shalt have no other gods before me." The Lord's prayer is parodied, with a significant inversion: instead of "*Thine* is the Kingdom, the Power, and the Glory," the new religion proclaims that "*Ours* is the kingdom, the power, and the glory." The rejection of transcendence is complete.

The attempts to go back to a pre-Hebraic spirituality and an organic, immanent religion meant a return to myth. Some Nazis actually attempted to restore the ancient paganism of the Germanic tribes. Göring officially recognized the ancient cultic sites. He promoted the revival of the winter solstice rituals from the old Germanic religions.[52] The Farmer's Almanac of 1935, published by the Ministry of Agriculture, went so far as to replace the Christian holidays with commemoration days for Wotan and Thor. Good Friday was replaced with a memorial day for those killed by Charlemagne in his efforts to convert the Saxons.[53]

Carl Jung perceptively, but with some sympathy, described Nazism as the revival of Wotan, who had been suppressed by Christianity but now was released. Germany was being possessed by its archetypal god.[54]

The rediscovery of primitive mythology characterized the whole modernist movement. The music and ballet of Stravinsky, the poetry of Yeats and Eliot, the fiction of Joyce, the psychology of Jung, all employed myth as a means of order and expression. Indeed, as will be discussed in chapter 7, many such modernists were, at least for awhile, attracted to fascism. Myth, with its depths of meaning and mystery, was an antidote to modern materialism, and, as Jung has suggested, a key to the inner life.

The recovery of a mythological consciousness meant the integration of the social, the spiritual, and the natural. Thus, alienation would be ended. This was the ultimate promise of fascism. The individual, healed of the fragmentation that characterizes the 20th century, would find wholeness and fulfillment in identity with nature and with the larger community. For the *German Christian* theologian Emanuel Hirsch, as one scholar summarizes his position, "myth in its immediate, irrational, enthusiastic power had helped the individual to endure the horrors of life even as it had provided a necessary religious foundation for the state."[55] But to fully return to myth meant that the whole Judeo-Christian heritage had to be demolished. That fascism revivified myth may explain its psychological appeal. It may also explain its barbarism and its madness.

Fascism and Modern Theology

Contemporary scholarship stresses the importance of contextualization. Ideas do not exist in isolation. They need to be placed into their historical context before they can be fully understood. It is surely significant that the major theologians of the 20th century were personally involved with the struggle over the German church. Moreover, the major issues of modern theology—Biblical authority, the status of traditional doctrines, the relation of church to culture—came to a head in the confrontation with fascism. And yet the significance of this struggle has, for the most part, been neglected by contemporary theology.

The confrontation with Hitler was an acid test for modern theology. Abstract ideas and academic speculations were suddenly subjected to actual life, to a concrete reality in which moral assumptions and religious beliefs once more became matters of life and death. The times demanded a commitment to one side or the other. The stakes were heightened by the knowledge that a commitment in one direction could bring the Gestapo. In the crucible of fascism, the implications and authenticity of a theological position could be tested.

This is not to advocate theological analysis ad hominem. There were misplaced allegiances, temporizing, inconsistency, and plain cowardice—as well as resistance and martyrdom—across the theological spectrum. The doctrine of original sin implies that human beings will never live up to their beliefs. The validity of a theological position must be established by argumentation and scholarship, not solely by the theologian's personal or political life.

But religion embraces life as well as thought, ethical action as well as abstract belief. Although we cannot judge a theology solely by the actions of particular believers, its impact upon life is part of its meaning. Religious belief manifests itself in the actual world. Hence, as Jesus said, speaking of false prophets, "You will know them by their fruits" (Matthew 7:16).

Today, it is difficult to evaluate ideas and beliefs because it is so difficult to establish a consensus of values. Most people, however shallow their knowledge, would agree that Hitler's regime was evil. This might provide a reference point for evaluation. The position of a thinker or a philosophy or a theory vis-à-vis fascism is thus highly relevant.

It is legitimate to ask what intellectual and religious trends helped to form fascist ideology and what positions proved most resistant. Whatever the extent of collaboration or resistance among particular church members, the theological struggle in the German church was between *syncretism* and *confessionalism.* Those who opposed Hitler on religious grounds did so on the basis of a *confessional* faith, that is, to belief in traditional Christian doctrines and to the authority of the Bible.

Consider these recurring themes of modern theology: the relationship between culture and Christianity; a "this-worldly" focus versus "other-worldly" salvationism; subjective experience versus objective doctrine; Biblical criticism versus Biblical authority. The debates over these issues developed throughout the 19th century, as fascist ideology was also taking form. In each case the "modernist" positions on these issues was also the position taken by the *German Christian* movement: the privileging of culture, the politicization of the Gospel, the minimizing of doctrine, the criticism of Biblical authority. Conversely, the Biblically orthodox positions became the basis of the *Confessional* movement: cultural iconoclasm; supernaturalism; doctrinal rigor; the authority of Scripture.

This is not to say that the *Confessing* church was fundamentalist. Barth's neoorthodoxy was not exactly the same as the orthodoxy of the past. Bonhoeffer articulated a radical modern theology of his own. The divisions between "crisis theologians" and conservatives,

70

as between Lutherans and Reformed, remained in the *Confessing* church. And yet, what seems most significant in the array of theologians and pastors who signed the Barmen declaration is their turn in time of crisis to *confessionalism,* to an assertion of transcendent Biblical truths. Such confessionalism, which in many ways goes against the mainstream of modern theology, was necessary to oppose "the practical and violent resistance to transcendence"[56] that was fascism.

As the Czech ally of the *Confessing* church Josef Hromadka wrote,

> The liberal theology in Germany and in her orbit utterly failed. It was willing to compromise on the essential points of divine law and of "the law of nature"; to dispose of the Old Testament and to accept the law of the Nordic race instead; and to replace the "Jewish" law of the Old Testament by the autonomous law of each race and nation respectively. It had made all the necessary preparation for the "Germanization of Christianity" and for a racial Church.[57]

And yet, this very tradition of liberal German theology continues to dominate mainline theology, as if the church struggle and the Holocaust never happened. As one Holocaust scholar has observed, "The lessons to be learned from the Church Struggle and the Holocaust have hardly penetrated our Protestant seminaries, our liberal Protestant press, our church literature, the thinking and writing of even our ablest older theologians."[58] He concludes, "American Liberal Protestantism is sick, and the theological form of its sickness can be summarized by saying that it stands solidly on ground but lately vacated by the 'German Christians'. . . who collaborated with Nazism."[59]

The politicization of the Gospel is a project of both liberals and conservatives in American Christianity. While biblical Christianity has a responsibility to bear witness to a transcendent ethic and on that basis to criticize social evils, the danger comes when that transcendent focus is lost and the church sells out to a secular ideology. Today the "crude salvationism" and "other-worldliness" of traditional religion are giving way to elaborate efforts to use Christianity to sanction a political agenda. Liberation theology promotes a socialist utopia; fundamentalists who follow "reconstructionism" pro-

71

mote a theocratic state. The *German Christians,* for the most part, would be able to agree with both of them.

The contemporary stress on *community* as the focus of church life is another good-sounding emphasis that in practice can become sinister, as the *German Christians* have shown. Communalism creates a group identity that can overwhelm any claims of the individual. This is especially true when that community is invested with a divine status. Certainly, a local congregation is to be a kind of community, but one made up of distinct individuals, as different from each other as the organs that make up one body (1 Corinthians 12). Too often, communalism leads instead to conformity and to the replacement of transcendent values with group values.

When that sense of community is transferred to a larger sphere, to a faction, to an ethnic group, we are closer to what the *German Christians* were seeking. Today, communities based on race, gender, and subculture (such as the "gay community"), are dominating the agendas of many mainline churches. The *German Christians* likewise defined community in terms of race, ethnicity, and culture. They then sanctioned nationalism by defining the nation as an ethnic community.

The philosophical irrationalism of contemporary religion is another point of continuity with the *German Christians.*[60] The eclipse of doctrine has meant in many circles an exclusive emphasis upon experience and subjectivity. Again, this is happening throughout American religion, among both liberals and fundamentalists, both inside and outside the church.

Religion becomes the pursuit of subjective experience, whether in manipulatively staged "worship experiences" or in pseudo-psychological small group encounters. The focus is not so much on the transcendent God, but on the self. What gives this kind of experience its religious flavor is that the self becomes caught up into a larger personality—not God, but the community. The sense of alienation is overcome when the individual is absorbed into the group. This is, of course, exactly the point and the appeal of fascism.

That religion is now thought of as an excursion into the irrational explains the peculiarities of popular religion. Many highly educated people now plan their lives by horoscopes, wear magic crystals to align their interplanetary energy, and consult channelers who claim to be possessed by space aliens. One wonders how anyone could believe that sort of thing. The answer is that the very irrationalism of such practices gives them their legitimacy. If reason leads to meaninglessness, then nonreason must be the source of meaning. The paraphernalia of New Age spirituality offers an ersatz mystical experience, without the demands of a transcendent faith. On a deeper level, it signals a return of myth and a revival of a distinctly pagan, pre-Judeo-Christian consciousness. Again, this is the point and the appeal of fascism.

The problem of all of these forms of irrationalism is that there are no longer any criteria for judgment. If there are no transcendent absolutes by which one can evaluate experiences or beliefs, then *any* experience or belief can be invested with a religious meaning. There is no basis for saying one idea is true and another false. There is no basis for insisting that a particular moral principle—for example, that one ought not murder Jews—is universally binding. This is why, in attempting to refute Nazism, the Christian resistance had to become *Confessional.*

Certainly, the contemporary church is far from fascism, at least for now. But the elements are there, perhaps awaiting a catalyst. In the 1970s, I happen to have been a member of the Disciples of Christ, a mainline liberal Protestant denomination. I remember hearing about a congregation in San Francisco that had an extremely effective inner-city ministry. Delegates to denominational meetings would attend workshops lauding this congregation's programs and lifting them up as examples for emulation. The congregation was called The People's Temple. Its pastor was a Disciples of Christ clergyman named Jim Jones. After leading his flock to Guyana, the Reverend Jim Jones arranged the murder of a U.S. Congressman, whereupon the whole congregation, at his command, committed suicide by drinking poisoned Kool-aid.

Once the Jonestown massacre hit the headlines, the denomination tried to distance itself from the Reverend Jim Jones and the People's Temple. Lacking a confessional framework, the church leaders admitted that they had no basis for disciplining Reverend Jones or for preventing his church from becoming a bizarre, dictatorial cult. But the People's Temple was a cult whose origins, unlike those centered in Eastern religion or fundamentalism, were in mainline Protestant theology.

The People's Temple was motivated by *Liberation theology.* Reverend Jones's socialist idealism demonized ordinary society and, like all other legalisms, invested its believers with a self-righteousness that could justify anything. This politicized Gospel was combined with an intense communalism. Encounter-group techniques—such as total self-exposure and submission to the group—were experimented with throughout the denomination, but the People's Temple pushed them to extremes to create an extraordinary unity and group solidarity. This absorption of the individual into the group manifested itself in unquestioning subjugation to Reverend Jones, the surrender of all property to the collective, the suppression of dissent, and the mass immigration to Guyana. Their group identity was so strong that mothers poisoned their own children when Reverend Jones told them to, and the whole congregation died with their arms around each other.

When the wellsprings of irrationalism are released, human beings have a tendency to lurch to authoritarianism, violence, and self-destruction. The confessional doctrine of original sin accounts for the way that laudable ideals and noble-sounding goals can so quickly turn monstrous. Certainly, this was the case in Jonestown. And in Nazi Germany.

The significance of Nazism does loom large in one school of contemporary theology: the *God-is-dead* movement. For the "Christian atheists," the magnitude of the Holocaust means that faith in a personal, loving God must be abandoned. His own people were slaughtered, and God did nothing. God's silence and inaction in the face of these horrors are a turning point in the history of religion. In the post-Holocaust age, God is dead. Transcendent religion must give way to a new kind of faith.

In the words of Thomas Altizer,

> If there is one clear portal to the 20th century, it is a passage through the death of God, the collapse of any meaning or reality lying beyond the newly discovered radical immanence of modern man, an immanence dissolving even the memory of the shadow of transcendence.[61]

The death of God, the movement holds, will lead to a new spirituality, one centered in the human and the immanent.

The death of God theologians, while taking the Holocaust seriously, may be—ironically and no doubt against their will—the most entangled in the fascist legacy. *The death of God* is a Nietz-schean slogan, and Nietzsche, as the next chapter will show, was the godfather of fascist ideology. Heidegger used the phrase in pro-claiming his project of Nazifying the university and German intel-lectual life: "The reality of the will to power can be expressed with Nietzsche, in the proposition 'God is dead.'" This does not mean ordinary atheism. Rather, it means that "the supersensible world," that is, the realm of the transcendent as associated with "the world of the Christian God," has lost its force and must be replaced.[62]

As has been shown, the personal, transcendent God of Judaism and Christianity was, to a large degree, the target of Nazi terror. God, along with the Jews, was the intended victim of the concen-tration camps. If the Holocaust means that God is really dead, then the Nazis were victorious indeed.

When Heidegger rejects "the supersensible world" in favor of a new spirituality centered in Being, and when Altizer sees as the locus of meaning the "radical immanence of modern man, an im-manence dissolving even the memory of the shadow of transcend-ence," they are in agreement with each other. They are also in agreement with the essence of fascism: "the practical and violent resistance to transcendence."[63]

The problem of evil—how a loving, all-powerful God could allow so much suffering—is as old as the Book of Job. The issue is theologically and spiritually profound, admitting neither glib solu-tions nor glib dismissals. In a symposium on the Holocaust, the radical Jewish theologian Richard Rubenstein gave a paper articu-lating the position that, after Auschwitz, God must be rejected. In a remarkable rejoinder, Elie Wiesel, a survivor of Auschwitz, expresses understanding for that line of thought, but observes:

> How strange that the philosophy denying God came not from the
> survivors. Those who came out with the so-called God is dead
> theology, not one of them had been in Auschwitz. Those who had
> never said it.[64]

The believers who actually suffered, Wiesel points out, continued to practice their faith, reciting the Talmud, saying their prayers, even in the concentration camp. It seems that the Biblical God makes Himself known not so much in success and victory but in failure and suffering; in Luther's words, not in a theology of glory, but in a theology of the cross.

Wiesel says that his own experience in the camps led him not so much to question God but to question man.

> Within the system of the concentration camp something very strange took place. The first to give in, the first to collaborate— to save their lives—were the intellectuals, the liberals, the humanists, the professors of sociology, and the like. Because suddenly their whole concept of the universe broke down. They had nothing to lean on.[65]

Those who had a transcendent belief were able to resist. Few communists, he said, gave in. Even fewer priests. And no rabbis.

Wiesel's comments are parallel to those attributed to another Jew, Albert Einstein:

> Having always been an ardent partisan of freedom, I turned to the Universities, as soon as the revolution broke out in Germany, to find the Universities took refuge in silence. I then turned to the editors of powerful newspapers, who, but lately in flowing articles, had claimed to be the faithful champions of liberty. These men, as well as the Universities, were reduced to silence in a few weeks. I then addressed myself to the authors individually, to those who passed themselves off as the intellectual guides of Germany, and among whom many had frequently discussed the question of freedom and its place in modern life. They are in their turn very dumb. Only the Church opposed the fight which Hitler was waging against liberty. Till then I had no interest in the Church, but now I feel great admiration and am truly attracted to the Church which had the persistent courage to fight for spiritual truth and moral freedom. I feel obliged to confess that I now admire what I used to consider of little value.[66]

The church, insofar as it stood upon its Confessions and the Word of God, had a basis for resisting evil and falsehood. Those holding more modern philosophies, when the pressure came, did not.

Uncritical acceptance of intellectual trends, political utopianism, the exaltation of culture, the triumph of the will, confidence in human systems, the relativity of values,—such notions are scarcely credible after Auschwitz. Such ideas, noble and liberating as they seem, ironically, manifested themselves in atrocity. The confident project of rejecting the transcendent and putting in its place an immanent spirituality based upon human culture, human self-sufficiency, and a unity with nature led, such is the flaw in the human condition, to the construction of Auschwitz. The Holocaust was indeed a turning point for religious faith, not because it makes faith in God impossible, but because it makes faith in human beings impossible. Nevertheless, the *church struggle* continues.

5

"The Triumph of the Will" Fascist Philosophy

[Preventing the collapse of the West] *depends solely on whether we, as a historical-spiritual people, still and once again will ourselves—or whether we no longer will ourselves. . . . But we do will that our people fulfill its historical mission. We do will ourselves.*

—Martin Heidegger, "Rectoral Address"[1]

When our liberty is lost we are compelled to serve sin: that is, we will sin and evil, *we speak* sin and evil, *we do* sin and evil.

—Martin Luther, "The Bondage of the Will"[2]

No one should doubt the intellectual sophistication of the National Socialists. Elie Wiesel discovered that, contrary to the myth that the Nazis were uneducated brutes, most of the killers of the death squads had college degrees, including some with Ph.D.s in philosophy, literature, and even theology.[3] Jaroslav Krejci likewise found that while fascist movements in general tend to draw heavily from the lower middle-class, in those countries where fascism has been most successful—namely, Italy and Germany—students and the university-educated were strongly represented.[4] One study of a local Nazi party organization shows that 43.3 percent were university students.[5]

Georg Lukács has observed that tracing the path to Hitler involves the name of nearly every major German philosopher since Hegel: Schopenhauer, Nietzsche, Dilthy, Simmel, Scheler, Heidegger, Jaspers, Weber.[6] That the Nazis emerged out of such a distinguished intellectual tradition should by no means discredit completely the achievements of these important thinkers. But ideas have consequences, and the ideas that led to Auschwitz deserve special scrutiny. This is especially true when those ideas, often adopted uncritically, are still in vogue.

Nietzsche, for example, is acknowledged to have been a major precursor to fascist ideology. Today, he is back in fashion on university campuses. Heidegger was an active, ideologically committed member of the Nazi party. His ideas continue to dominate contemporary philosophy and hermeneutics. To be sure, Nietzsche and Heidegger were great philosophers, and their Nazi connections should not cast doubt on all of their insights. But it is surely important, in light of Auschwitz, to understand those elements of their thought that did correspond to Nazism and to determine whether those elements are part of their continuing influence. Responses to recent discoveries about Heidegger's Nazi activities have tended to either attack or to defend the great philosopher in personal terms. The real issue is often neglected: the relationship between fascism and existentialism.

The overcoming of the Judeo-Christian worldview and its ethic was achieved by a long intellectual and cultural process. It neither began nor ended with the Third Reich. The great filmmaker Leni Riefenstahl, one of many pro-Nazi artists, entitled her documentary tribute to Hitler, by his order, *The Triumph of the Will*. The phrase encapsulates the philosophy of fascism. Although Hitler's triumph was turned into a military defeat, the triumph of the will continues in contemporary philosophy, ethics, and culture.

"The crisis in Western culture was (and is)," according to David Hirsch, "the ease with which Europe was Nazified."[7] That Nazism took power so easily, with so little initial resistance, proves that it fit well with the climate of the time, that it was in tune with and a product of 20th-century European thought. Modern thought is usually presented and studied as an unbroken continuum of progress to the present day. But surely the Nazi debacle shows some deficiency in the modern tradition.

Soon after the end of World War II, the Jewish scholar Max Weinreich published *Hitler's Professors: The Part of Scholarship in Germany's Crimes against the Jewish People*. This exhaustive study of the complicity of German intellectuals with the Nazi regime documents how the scholarship of the time provided the intellectual justification and the conceptual framework for the Holocaust. This is not to say that these intellectuals necessarily intended the Holocaust, but, argues Weinreich, it would not have been possible without them. "Did they administer the poison?" he asks. "By no means; they only wrote the prescription."[8] He goes on to ask, "Is the germ of Nazidom destroyed . . . with the crushing of the Nazi state? Can [such] scholarship even if technically de-Nazified, be made an instrument of reeducating the German people?"[9]

Weinreich points out that the academics who supported Hitler, directly or indirectly, were sophisticated thinkers and distinguished experts in their fields. Their problem was not sham scholarship, but the "value-free" assumptions with which they pursued their research. Their "weakness is due not to inferior training but to the mendacity inherent in any scholarship that overlooks or openly repudiates all moral and spiritual values."[10]

Existentialism and Fascism

On the surface, existentialism would seem to be, if anything, the opposite of fascism. A philosophy of radical freedom centered in the individual is surely incompatible with a totalitarian social system that denies political liberty in the name of the community. Existentialism is generally seen as a philosophy of rebellion against all external authority. Nevertheless, the connections between existentialism and fascism are undeniable. Both movements trace their lineage to Nietzsche. While Sartre and Camus were part of the French resistance, the other major existentialist philosopher, Martin Heidegger, was an activist in the Nazi party.

What existentialism did was to challenge the traditional view that meaning inheres in the realm of the transcendent. According to existentialism, trusting some preordained system, some supposedly objective truth—whether moral, theological, or rational—is to find absurdity. Meaning does not lie in the realm of ideals or abstractions, but in one's personal existence. Meaning is personal. Life has no meaning, in the sense of some ready-made plan just waiting to be discovered. Human beings must create their own meaning. Although most people evade the responsibility for their own lives by succumbing to the preset forms set by others, authentic individuals will, by their choices and actions, create meaning for themselves.

80

Since existentialism, by its nature, refuses to give objective answers to moral or ideological questions, a particular existentialist might choose to follow either a democratic or a totalitarian ideology. Existentialism will not solve a person's political dilemma with some ready-made principles of its own. At issue is not the content of the choice—whether a person becomes a fascist or a member of the resistance—but whether the person made a genuine choice, taking full responsibility for the commitment that was made.[11]

But existentialism is more than an ideologically neutral methodology. By rejecting the concept of transcendent meaning, truth, and moral law, and by investing ultimate authority in the human will, existentialism played into the hands of fascism, which preached the same doctrines. If fascism can be defined as "the violent and practical resistance to transcendence,"[12] its affinities with existentialism are clear.

While not all of the tenets of various existentialist thinkers are compatible with fascism, the two movements are part of the same stream of thought, the late-romantic reaction against transcendence. Furthermore, the metaphysical and ethical implications of existentialism were often turned to the service of fascist theory.

Nietzsche

The genealogy of both existentialism and fascism goes back to Nietzsche. To be sure, Nietzsche rejected German nationalism, allegiance to the State, party membership, and racial anti-Semitism. These would become important to German National Socialism, though not necessarily to other fascist movements. But those who defend Nietzsche against the charge that he influenced fascism on the grounds that he was not a racist or a conformist misunderstand what fascism was all about.

As Nolte says, Nietzsche "was the first to give voice to that spiritual focal point toward which all fascism must gravitate: the assault on practical *and* theoretical transcendence, for the sake of a 'more beautiful life.' "[13] Nietzsche turned romanticism in a fascist direction. His rebelliousness would no doubt have brought him into conflict with the Nazi bureaucracy, once the party came to power; but his defiant pose was widely imitated in the initial fascist revolution. Nietzsche was not a racial anti-Semite, but he was an intellectual

81

anti-Semite, castigating the Jews for their ideas and their ethics, particularly as they manifest themselves in Christianity. Nietzsche's counter-ethic of power and cruelty was seized upon by SS members and concentration camp guards.

Nietzsche's thought demonstrates clearly how existentialist philosophy could lead to fascist policies. His critique of the Judeo-Christian tradition and the alternative ethic that he devised would become central to fascist theory. As one Nazi functionary said, whoever says "Heil Hitler!" at the same time is saluting Nietzsche's philosophy.[14]

At the heart of Nietzsche's philosophy is his contempt for abstractions. In his desire to affirm this life, he rejected the transcendental categories of reason and morality. Nietzsche held that abstraction of life comes from abstraction of thought. In Nolte's terms, the life-negating synthesis of theoretical transcendence (the focus on nonmaterial ideas) and practical transcendence (the impingement of these ideas on actual life) is morality. Nietzsche blamed Christianity, a creation of the Jews, for the denial of life manifested in morality. The other moralisms, such as democracy and socialism, are merely secular versions of Judeo-Christian guilt.[15]

Nietzsche was fearless in pursuing the implications of his assumptions. In his critique of Judeo-Christian morality, he attacked the Christian value of love. Notions of compassion and mercy, he argued, favor the weak and the unfit, thereby breeding more weakness. Nature is less sentimental, but ultimately kinder, in allowing the weak to die off. The ideals of Christian benevolence cause the unfit to flourish, while those who *are* fit are burdened by guilt and are coerced by the moral system to serve those who are beneath them.

Judaism and Christianity, according to Nietzsche, represent "the revolt of the slaves."[16] With Moses, the slaves of Egypt rose up against their superior Egyptian masters. With Christianity, the teachings of a crucified Galilean had such an appeal to the downtrodden of the Roman Empire—to women, slaves, outcasts, and the defeated—that classical civilization itself was overthrown. Whereas Marx believed that religion was a way the powerful could keep the underclasses under control, Nietzsche believed the opposite, that Christianity was a means by which the powerless—by manipulating guilt, requiring benevolence, and suppressing natural vitality—could enchain the powerful. Nietzsche idolized classical antiquity, with its celebration of strength, its unashamed sensuality, and its tough-minded acceptance of death. The Jews and the Christians, though, brought, in his words, "the gospel preached to the poor and base, the general revolt of all the downtrodden, the wretched, the failures, the less favored."[17] From this successful revolution of the unfit issued eventually the French revolution, democracy, the emancipation of women, socialism, and other manifestations of what Nietzsche saw as the total decadence of society.[18]

Nature, however, would not long be denied. In the modern world, according to Nietzsche, "God is dead."[19] Energizing conflict will reemerge. Human beings will continue to evolve. Man will give way to Superman. For Nietzsche, this next stage of human evolution is not merely a superior biological specimen, but a newly authentic self, who will usher in a new moral, cultural, and spiritual order. The Superman will not accept the abstract, transcendental meanings imposed by a disembodied rationalism or by a life-denying religion. Rather, the Superman will *create* meaning for himself and for the world as a whole.

The Superman, according to Nietzsche, is an artist who can shape the human race according to his will. "Man is for him an un-form, a material, an ugly stone that needs a sculptor."[20] Such a statement anticipates the eugenics movement as it would be formulated by the Nazis. Perhaps more significantly, it demonstrates how the exaltation of the will could lead not to general liberty, as one might expect, but to the control of the many by the elite, with those of weak will being subjugated to the will of the Supermen.

Morally, the Superman will be the polar opposite of the Judeo-Christian ideal, in which "acting human" implies kindness, compassion, empathy, and other "humane" traits. The Superman, in contrast, will be cruel:

> If his [the Superman's] strength rank still higher in the hierarchy
> . . . , it is not sufficient for him to be capable of cruelty merely at
> the *sight* of much suffering, perishing, and destruction: such a man
> must be capable of himself creating pain and suffering and ex-
> perience pleasure in so doing, he must be cruel in hand and deed
> (and not merely with the eyes of the spirit).[21]

Nietzsche's apologists tend to dismiss such statements as if they were mere debating points and attempts to shock the bourgeoisie, as if he did not intend them literally. But Nietzsche, in rejecting abstractionism and theoretical transcendence, was never interested in mere theory. His focus on the concrete requires not just ideas but action. This is in fact exactly the point of the passage: one must be cruel not only in theory but "in hand and deed."

Nietzsche's ethic of cruelty became the rationale for all of the Nazi atrocities. According to Nietzsche, "The weak and the failures shall perish: the first principle of *our* love of man. And they shall even be given every possible assistance. What is more harmful than any vice? Active pity for all the failures and the weak: Christianity."[22] This statement exemplifies another legacy of Nietzsche for the Nazis. What might be called the Nietzschean attitude—the flippant, sarcastic contempt for ordinary human values—is aped by nearly all of the fascist writers, from Adolf Hitler to Ezra Pound.

Nietzsche's influence on fascism is direct and complete. Besides his spiritual and moral stance, Nietzsche's cultural critique, his philosophical irrationalism, and his project of recovering the mythological consciousness are all taken over into fascist theory and rhetoric. J. Stroup summarizes the elements of fascist cultural theory that were taken from Nietzsche:

> Here are all the components in this system of cultural criticism: first, a cycle of cultural decay and rebirth, youth and age fluctuating according to closeness to the timeless eternity of irrational and ecstatically compelling myth (a view which fosters elitist hostility to rationality); second, the premise that all domains of culture— art, government, religion—are linked together and hence bound to flourish or decay according to a culture's place on the eternal roller coaster of closeness to and separation from the eternal, mythic springtime; third, ultimate significance given to aesthetic criteria at the price of moral absolutes; fourth, salvation conceived of as within the world rather than coming from outside it—Dionysos versus the Crucified.[23]

Nietzsche's apologists are quick to disassociate him from fascism, arguing that he would have been appalled with Hitler and the National Socialists. This may be, but there is no doubt that Hitler and the National Socialists embraced Nietzsche and considered themselves his disciples.

84

Heidegger

Later existentialism is more benign than that of Nietzsche, generally asserting more humane values. Nevertheless, Nietzsche's philosophy underlies all of the later existentialists, and the darker implications of his thought are difficult to avoid. Heidegger did not avoid them, committing himself to the National Socialist program, although, filtered through Heidegger, Nietzsche's ideas seem much more palatable.

Heidegger invokes Nietzsche in his "Rectoral Address," the speech he made upon accepting the rectorship of the University of Freiburg, in which he articulates his commitment to the integration of academia and National Socialism. If Nietzsche is correct in saying that "God is dead," Heidegger asks, what are the implications for knowledge? Heidegger says that we must take Nietzsche, "that passionate seeker of God," seriously in this regard and recognize the forsakenness of modern human beings." If God is dead, there is no longer a transcendent authority or reference point for objective truth. Whereas classical thought, exemplified by the Greeks, could confidently search for objective truth, today, after the death of God, truth becomes intrinsically "hidden and uncertain." Today the process of questioning is "no longer merely a preliminary step that is surmounted on the way to the answer and thus to knowing; rather, questioning itself becomes the highest form of knowing."[24]

Heidegger's conclusion has become accepted to the point of becoming a commonplace of contemporary thought, *that knowledge is a matter of process, not content.* With the death of God, there is no longer a set of absolutes or abstract ideals by which existence must be ordered. Such "essentialism" is an illusion; knowledge in the sense of objective, absolute truth must be challenged. The scholar is not the one who knows or searches for some absolute truth, but the one who questions everything that pretends to be true.

Such a view is a corollary of existential metaphysics, that there is no transcendentally valid meaning. Heidegger's replacement of knowledge with questioning has been taken up by educational theorists (who minimize the teaching of content in favor of teaching processes), theologians such as Paul Tillich (for whom faith involves constantly questioning rather than believing in doctrines), and now the typical man on the street who is likely to agree that "there are no absolutes" and "truth is relative."

One would think that such a skeptical methodology would be highly incompatible with fascism, with its practice of subjecting people to an absolute human authority. And yet this betrays a misunderstanding of fascism. Heidegger's "Rectoral Address" was warmly praised by his fellow National Socialists. The fascists saw themselves as iconoclasts, interrogating the old order and boldly challenging all transcendent absolutes. That they themselves were authoritarians and forbade counter-questioning must not have seemed inconsistent.

Thus, in the same address in which he asserts that "questioning itself becomes the highest form of knowing," Heidegger goes on to advocate expelling academic freedom from the university: "To give oneself the law is the highest freedom. The much-lauded 'academic freedom' will be expelled from the university." Heidegger argues that the traditional canons of academic freedom are not genuine but only negative, encouraging "lack of concern" and "arbitrariness." Scholars must become unified with each other and devote themselves to service. In doing so, "the concept of the freedom of German students is now brought back to its truth."[25] The claim that freedom will emerge when academic freedom is eliminated is sophistry of the worst kind. But Heidegger's statement is more than rhetorical doublespeak.

Heidegger is speaking existentially, calling not for blind obedience, but for a genuine commitment of the will. Freedom is preserved because "to give oneself the law" is a voluntary, freely chosen commitment. Academic freedom as the disinterested pursuit of truth shows "arbitrariness," partaking of the old essentialist view that truth is objective and transcendent. The essentialist scholar is detached and disengaged, showing "lack of concern," missing the sense in which truth is ultimately personal, a matter of the will, demanding personal responsibility and choice. In the new order, the scholar will be fully engaged in service to the community. Academic freedom is alienating, a function of the old commitment to moral and intellectual absolutes.

The concept that there are no absolute truths means that human beings can impose *their* truth upon an essentially meaningless world. There are no objective, essentialist criteria to stand in the way of united, purposeful scholars forging their new intellectual order and willing the essence of the German people. What this meant in practice can be seen in the Bavarian Minister of Culture's directive to professors in Munich, that they were no longer to determine whether something "is true, but whether it is in keeping with the direction of the National Socialist revolution."[26]

The nature of Heidegger's complicity with the Nazis is hotly debated.[27] His apologists claim that he was naive, being too easily swayed by the fascist promises. At worst, they say, he was opportunistic, taking advantage of the new regime to further his ambitions in academic politics. Victor Farias, on the other hand, has marshalled recent evidence to show that Heidegger was on his way to becoming "*the* philosopher of the Third Reich."[28]

Eventually, Heidegger did fall out of favor and had to give up his rectorate, not, however, out of enlightened opposition to fascism but because he came out on the losing side of a major ideological battle within the Nazi party. As Farias shows, in aligning himself with the Storm Troopers of Ernst Röhm and insisting on persecuting Catholic student groups, Heidegger was considered too radical even for Hitler.[29]

One of the issues in this party schism was the role of biological racism as advocated by Alfred Rosenberg. Röhm, with Heidegger, downplayed racial determinism and advocated something closer to Mussolini's fascism, stressing a "continuous revolution" of economic socialism and violent cultural change. Heidegger's apologists cite evidence that he was no racist, but this means only that he was on the side of Röhm rather than Rosenberg.

Röhm's Storm Troopers (SA, for *Sturmabteilung*, "Assault Divisions") were the Brown Shirts, the paramilitary civilian corps of street fighters and terrorists which were so instrumental in Hitler's rise to power. By 1933, The SA boasted over 2 million members, twice the size of the army, including various student and university organizations with which Heidegger was involved. (The SA is to be distinguished from the SS [*Schutzstaffel*, "Defense Echelons"]. The SS were the Black Shirts, who constituted the secret police [the Gestapo], Hitler's bodyguards, various military divisions, and the concentration camp guards.) The SA may have been less interested in racial theory, but they were even more extreme in their advocacy of violence and suppression, against not only Jews but also against

Aryans who represented the old order. Röhm was resolutely opposed by the more conservative wing of the Nazi party, particularly by the army (which Röhm wanted to integrate with his Storm Troopers). Himmler, head of the SS, also feared Röhm, with his rival civilian power base outside of his centralized control. In this major ideological struggle for control of the party, Hitler, to avoid social upheaval and to placate the army, came down on the side of Rosenberg and against his old comrade Röhm. On June 30, 1934, after a rumor of an attempted uprising on the part of the SA, Hitler had Röhm executed without trial, beginning "the night of the long knives," a purge in which at least 177 radicals were murdered.[30] After the purge, the SS, which was established on racial and eugenic lines, assumed the power formerly held by the SA. In this bloody realignment of the Nazi party, Heidegger was fortunate to lose only his rectorate.[31]

Nevertheless, Heidegger remained a loyal Nazi. Farias reports that Heidegger would begin and end each lecture with the Nazi salute ("Heil Hitler!") even after it was no longer obligatory, as Heidegger had made it when he was rector.

The important issue, of course, is not Heidegger's life but his thought. To argue that Heidegger's ideas are not true simply because Heidegger was a Nazi is to commit the ad hominem fallacy. The problem is that there are genuine, foundational affinities between Heidegger's existentialism and the ideology of National Socialism. Despite the genius of *Being and Time*, Farias shows how many of its concepts acquire a more sinister resonance in light of Nazi ideology: "categories like the We, struggle, destiny, the historical mandate of the people, community, and, above all, the exemplary leader, who in this situation is expected to point out the path that the people will follow."[32] Taken as a whole and placing Heidegger's ideas in a historical context, it is difficult to avoid the conclusion of David Hirsch: "Much as it may pain philosophers to admit it, Hitler and Heidegger shared a world outlook. Both sought to return German culture to pagan roots by rupturing that fusion between Hellenism and Hebraism that constitutes European humanism."[33]

Hirsch acutely recognizes Heidegger's affinity with the fascists as lying in their common reaction against the Judeo-Christian tradition:

Though Hitler hated Jews and would have been prepared to exterminate them on the basis of his hatred alone, he also hated them as the originators of Christianity, which he, like Nietzsche, found to be a decadent religion. Can we overlook the fact that Heidegger's undermining of metaphysics and his desire to burrow his way back to a pre-Socratic revelation of Being by means of the German language is a philosophical parallel to Hitler's political agenda of returning to a pre-biblical, pre-Christian past?[34]

Heidegger's Jewish contemporaries interpreted his thought in exactly these terms. A Jewish periodical published a response to Heidegger's "Rectoral Address," which defined the issues precisely: "Heroic nationalism, 'cooperative knowledge of the nation,' is the ultimate meaning of life for Heidegger. This [is a] barrier against the kingdom of values and its transcendental roots in God."[35]

Heidegger's analysis of "Being," and his speculations about "the hidden" that underlies subjectivity, his reflections on meaning, language, and hermeneutics are valuable and profound. But his efforts to replace transcendence with immanence merged easily with those of fascism. This is evident in Heidegger's concept of the spiritual: As he says in the "Rectoral Address," the realm of the spiritual is not some objective superstructure of a culture, nor is it a storehouse of objective information and transcendent values. Rather, a people's spiritual world "is the force of the deepest preservation of its powers of earth and blood."[36] The spiritual is not a matter of objective knowledge and moral values, much less transcendent religious truth; the spiritual has to do with earth, blood, and power.

The Will

In rejecting transcendent meaning, existentialism insists that meaning is created by the human will. Nietzsche bases his whole philosophy and ethic on the exaltation of "the will to power."[37] Later existentialists toned down Nietzsche's emphasis upon power (an emphasis that would be resurrected in postmodern thought), but the will as the originator of authentic meaning remains central. Thus, an important concept for Heidegger is "willing the essence." In the "Rectoral Address," Heidegger calls on the university to come together into a common will and to will its essence—that is, to will knowledge and to will its historical and spiritual mission.[38] When

Heidegger speaks in this way of "willing the essence," he is keeping the existentialist dictum that existence precedes essence.[39] There is no preexisting essence to which individuals must conform. Essence comes into being when it is willed.

Heidegger is referring not only to the will of the individual but also to a "common" or collective will. As Rousseau had also emphasized, those who will the same thing constitute a community, which takes on a life and a will of its own. In *Being and Time*, Heidegger argues that individuals can achieve full authenticity only by participation in such a community, which does not erase personal identity but gives it fulfillment: "Authentic existence becomes secure within the context of a communal life, from which the loss of personal identity is entirely excluded."[40]

The existentialists' emphasis upon the will, and thus human freedom, seems to fly in the face of fascist totalitarianism. Yet the will—and even calls for freedom—played a prominent role in fascist theory and rhetoric. "Of the highest importance," writes Hitler in *Mein Kampf*, "is the training of will-power and determination, plus the cultivation of joy in responsibility."[41] The centrality of the will means that those who choose must take responsibility for their fate, a common theme of existentialism. "The aim of a German foreign policy of today," writes Hitler, "must be the preparation for the reconquest of freedom for tomorrow."[42]

Hitler is referring to a collective will, in addition to the isolated will of the individual, and to national freedom, rather than freedom of individuals. Fascists believed in communalism, in which the individual's will and freedom finds fulfillment in the will and freedom of the group. The goal was not mindless conformity, but masses of individuals all actively willing the same thing.

If reason can no longer lead to a common truth and if meaning is a function of the will, then the intellectual life becomes a conflict of competing wills. Persuasion is a matter not of rationally analyzing evidence to reach a common conclusion; rather, it becomes a matter of power, of one will conquering other wills.

In a discussion of his political rallies, Hitler analyzes persuasion as the process whereby weak wills are overwhelmed by a stronger will:

In all these cases [of public oratory] we have to do with an encroachment upon man's freedom of will. This applies most, of course, to meetings attended by people with a contrary attitude of will, who must now be won over to a new will. In the morning and even during the day people's will power seems to struggle with the greatest energy against an attempt to force upon them a strange will and a strange opinion. At night, however, they succumb more easily to the dominating force of a stronger will. For, in truth, every such meeting represents a wrestling bout between two opposing forces. The superior oratorical art of a dominating preacher will succeed more easily in winning to the new will people who have themselves experienced a weakening of their force of resistance in the most natural way than those who are still in full possession of their mental tension and will.[43]

Fascist rhetoric thus aims at the will rather than the mind. Rational discussion is replaced with psychological and rhetorical manipulation; the search for truth is set aside in favor of a power struggle and a contest of wills.

That fascism placed such an importance on the will may help to explain its particular mode of tyranny. Those who dissented with the regime were seen not as people who disagreed intellectually or philosophically, but as people with hostile wills. In rejecting the common will, they were guilty of not belonging. This is perhaps why the Nazi apparatus was so thorough in its interrogations—what was wanted was not so much conformity but assent. Those who disagreed were exhibiting a contrary will; they were not skeptics but enemies. Conflicts of the will cannot be mediated by reason; they can only be resolved by force, with one will imposing itself on the other. There is no question of persuasion; only coercion or— for those totally outside the collective will, such as Jews—elimination.

Perhaps the greatest example of fascist art is Leni Riefenstahl's film *The Triumph of the Will*. Her documentary of the Nuremberg rally of the National Socialist Party is more than a *tour de force* of propaganda; it is a brilliantly-crafted and revealing expression of fascist ideas and values. Riefenstahl's title alludes to Nietzsche's concept of "the will to power." Significantly, the title was provided to her by Hitler himself.[44] The film presents the accession of Hitler as a triumph of his indomitable will as embodying the collective will of the German people. Riefenstahl takes documentary footage and edits it into a mythic narrative. Hitler's arrival at Nuremberg by plane is portrayed as the descent of a god from the skies. The spectacle of this god being received by his people, in mass adoration and formal ritual, is stunning in its mythic impact.

The Nietzschean and Nazi phrase *the triumph of the will* has another resonance. It alludes to and inverts another monumental text of German culture: *The Bondage of the Will* by Martin Luther. This particular book was Luther's *magnum opus*, often considered the manifesto of the Reformation.[45] Luther was a cultural hero to the Germans, lauded not only for his religious revolution but for his role in solidifying the German language and defining the German nation. In simultaneously alluding to Luther and contradicting him, *The Triumph of the Will* invests Hitler with Luther's mantle and replaces German Protestantism with the new fascist spirituality. (When Hitler's informal conversations were later recorded and collected, they were published under the same title as Luther's: *Table Talk*.)[46] Hitler has been described as an anti-Christ; he placed himself in the role of an anti-Luther. Although some scholars have blamed Luther for various qualities in German culture that made it susceptible to Nazism, the contrast between *The Triumph of the Will* and *The Bondage of the Will* is absolute.[47]

According to Luther, the will is in bondage to sin. The fallen will is enslaved to Satan and, if left to itself, will choose what is evil. The human will is perversely set against the righteous will of God. For sinful human beings, the will is not in a state of liberty but is in bondage to its worst impulses. "When our liberty is lost we are compelled to serve sin: that is, we *will* sin and evil, we *speak* sin and evil, we *do* sin and evil."[48] Whereas medieval Catholicism taught that human beings can come to God by the exercise of their wills, Luther taught that the human will of itself can only reject God. This primal alienation from God is a willful rebellion, and the source of all subsequent evil:

> Nor is it an inconsiderable assertion, when man is said to be ignorant of, and to despise God: for these are the fountain springs of all evils. What evil is there not, where there are ignorance and contempt of God? In a word, the whole kingdom of Satan in men, could not be defined in fewer or more expressive words than by the saying—they are ignorant of and despise God! For there is unbelief, there is disobedience, there is sacrilege, there is blas-

phemy against God, there is cruelty and a want of mercy towards
our neighbour, there is the love of self in all the things of God
and man!—Here you have a description of the glory and power
of "Free-will!"[49]

Salvation comes not from the human will but from the will of God,
who intervenes and enters into the human condition in Christ, offering salvation freely by grace. In Christ, as mediated by the sacraments and the Word of the Gospel, the bondage is broken, the
sinful will is remade, and human beings are liberated.[50]

Luther's critique of the will is grounded in the Bible, with its
assertion of God's transcendent law and the failure of human beings
to keep that law. If the human will is unleashed, with no external
or internal restraints, Luther would expect not authenticity, not self-
actualization or humanistic fulfillment, but an evil approaching the
demonic. In this respect, at least, those who celebrated the *triumph
of the will* proved him right.

6

"Life Unworthy of Life"
Fascist Ethics

Of the five identifiable steps by which the Nazis carried out the principle of "life unworthy of life," coercive sterilization was the first. There followed the killing of "impaired" children in hospitals; and then the killing of "impaired adults," mostly collected from mental hospitals, in centers especially equipped with carbon monoxide gas. This project was extended (in the same killing centers) to "impaired" inmates of concentration and extermination camps and, finally, to mass killings, mostly of Jews, in the extermination camps themselves.

—Robert Jay Lifton, *The Nazi Doctors* (1986)[1]

Justice is what the Aryan man deems just. Unjust is what he so deems.

—Reichsminister Alfred Rosenberg[2]

Mere cruelty cannot explain the death camps. The very logistics of mass extermination required rational planning, technological ingenuity, and sophisticated management. The most chilling aspect of the Holocaust, besides the suffering of its victims, is the cold-bloodedness of those who carried it out, who seemed incapable of normal human feelings such as empathy, pity, or guilt.

The mind-set that could consign men, women, and children, whole families, whole races, to the gas chambers was philosophically conditioned. Those who operated the death camps and those who tolerated them or created the climate that allowed them to come into being were guilty of both a moral failure and an ethical failure. That is, their immoral actions were predicated upon their philosophy of right and wrong. Their moral principles were shaped by their worldview.

The rejection of the Judeo-Christian ethic of transcendent moral absolutes meant that concepts such as justice and mercy no longer had a conceptual foundation. In place of such ethical abstractions, the fascists formulated an immanent ethic, grounded in the needs of the community and having its origins in the strength of the human will. "Conscience," said Hitler, "is a Jewish invention."[3] The Jewish prophets and the confessional Christians could have predicted what would happen when conscience is silenced, objective morality is dismantled, and the only moral authority becomes the fallen human will: the monumental eruption of human depravity.

The apotheosis of the will meant that the Judeo-Christian ethic of compassion would be replaced by a new ethic based on the values of strength and power. This manifested itself in the glorification of violence and in the sanctioning of eugenics, euthanasia, and finally genocide.

Existential Ethics

Existential ethics is centered not upon moral absolutes but upon the individual's moral choice. An action is praiseworthy not in terms of whether or not it conforms to some external moral code, but whether or not it reflects a genuine choice and commitment on the part of the individual. In Heidegger's terms, those who blindly conform to other people's rules are *inauthentic.* They deny their own responsibility for their lives and reject their innate freedom, letting other people make their decisions for them. Those who freely choose a course of action, asserting their will to shape their own lives, are *authentic.* Whether they choose traditional morality or a more unconventional lifestyle, what validates their action is whether or not there was a conscious choice.

Existential ethics, far from being the province of academic and obscure philosophers, has come to dominate contemporary moral discourse, even in popular culture. The debates, for example, on abortion show the collision between the existential way of approaching ethical issues and the Judeo-Christian approach. The latter seeks absolute moral principles, such as the Biblical injunction "Thou shalt not kill" and the transcendent value of human life. The question remains whether or not a developing fetus is an example of human life and therefore worthy of protection. Objective evidence is admitted at this point, whether from Scripture or from medicine, as well as rational discussion about the definition of human life.

Existential ethics brackets the objective issues on abortion entirely. At issue is not some transcendent moral law, nor medical evidence, nor logical analysis. The *only* issue is whether or not the mother has a choice. The content of that choice makes no difference. If the mother chooses to have the baby, her action is moral. If she chooses not to have the baby, her action is still moral. If she has no choice in the matter—if she bears a child against her will or aborts a child against her will—then and only then is the action evil. (While she may be guilty of an inauthentic conformity to society's expectations, more likely the fault lies with those who have taken away her freedom.) Those who believe that abortion should be legal do not consider themselves "pro-abortion." They are "pro-choice." The term is not only a rhetorical euphemism but a precise definition of existential ethics.

Existentialism is also reflected in those who are "pro-choice" but personally oppose abortion. They do not believe in abortion for themselves, but refuse to impose their beliefs on others. In this view, a belief has no validity outside the private, personal realm of each individual. Moral and religious beliefs are no more than personal constructions, important in giving meaning to an individual's life, but not universally valid. Or, to use another commonly accepted axiom, "what's true for you may not be true for me."

Such a view of truth flies in the face of all classical metaphysics, which sees truth as objective, universal, and applicable to all. Truth may be known only partially and it may elude human knowledge, to one degree or another, but theoretically, if a proposition is true, it is true for everyone. The now popular notion that truth is relative shows the surprisingly strong impact of the seemingly arcane philosophy of existentialism on contemporary popular culture.

"Values Clarification" exercises, which constitute the major methodology of contemporary ethical education, are also applications of existentialist ethics.[4] An imaginary ethical dilemma is described. ("Your bomb shelter has room for only ten people. You have 20 people in your neighborhood: a scientist, an artist, a teenage boy, a fashion model, a doctor, a pro-football player, a 70-year old man, a woman hooked up to a respirator, the neighborhood grouch, a pastor, a baby. . . .There is a nuclear attack. Whom do you let into your fallout shelter? Whom do you let live, and whom do you let die?") Students then "choose" what they would do. There are no right answers. The purpose is to clarify what values the student already has and to force them into—another existential catch-phrase—"ethical decision-making."

A traditional moralist would object that the scenarios are intrinsically immoral, since they are artificially contrived so that some evil will result no matter what action is chosen. Perhaps more seriously, they force the student into a role that is itself morally problematic ("whom do you let die?"). Impossible moral dilemmas, presented without any guiding principles, are not the best vehicles for moral education, which traditionally seeks to inculcate objective values, such as justice and compassion. Such dilemmas might be debated by sophisticated thinkers, armed with the wisdom of the ages, but they teach children only that moral questions are never clear-cut, and that whatever they *choose* is right.

Situation ethics, first formulated by the existentialist theologian Joseph Fletcher, now pervades the entire culture. This approach to ethics focuses not upon applying moral absolutes, but upon responsible decision-making based upon the unique circumstances of each situation. In this view, stealing might be morally valid, if it is the self-less action of a man trying to feed his family. Adultery may be good, if it helps a woman come to terms with her sexuality. Killing one's father may be a moral act, if he is only being kept alive by a machine. Traditional moralists would say that situation ethics is only pretending to avoid moral absolutes. Feeding one's family, sexual needs, and "the quality of life" are in fact being treated as objective values that are simply being held up as superior to traditional moral values. But *situation ethics* does operate differently by stressing the choice of the individual and by turning to values that come out of the individual's experience. Personal ties, "felt needs," the avoidance of suffering—such values are very different from the stern, self-denying demands of the Judeo-Christian ethic. Situation ethics replaces transcendent values with immanent values.

Although it purports to judge each situation individually, the application of situation ethics remains fairly predictable. All sexual behavior—as long as there is consent—will be sanctioned. A situation ethicist will, of course, be pro-choice when it comes to abortion. It is very difficult for situation ethics to condemn suicide, since by definition, the person chooses to die. All advocates of situation ethics endorse euthanasia.

Today, sexual freedom, abortion, and euthanasia are widely accepted. Suicide is seen more as a tragedy than a moral evil, and it is widely approved of if the person is terminally ill. Before the 20th century, though, suicide, euthanasia, and abortion were seen as horrible evils, and sexual behavior was regulated by strict moral guidelines. While people have always committed adultery, they have never before argued that it could be moral to do so. To go from the sexual restrictions of the previous centuries to the sexual permissiveness of today signals a monumental ethical revolution. The change, I would argue, is away from the Judeo-Christian ethic of transcendental moral absolutes to an existential ethic of immanent values ratified by the will.

When the existential ethic becomes the basis not only for personal moral stances but for public policy, it sometimes loses its humane appearance. In values clarification exercises, the Doomsday scenario, as with most of the moral quandaries used in values clarification, encourages a cold-bloodedly pragmatic approach to moral thinking. Usually, the aged and the handicapped get left out of the fallout shelter. ("The old man has already lived his life and the woman on the machine would be too big a burden for the others to take care of.") Unpractical types such as pastors and artists and those who would not fit in with the community of the survivors also tend to get the door shut in their faces. The prime values become *social utility* (the doctor and the scientist usually make the cut) and *strength* (teenagers, athletes, and healthy young people in the prime of life are always welcome). The same sort of moral reasoning and ethical decision-making was practiced in Nazi Germany with similar conclusions.

Ethics without Principles

As Robert Ericksen has observed, "In terms of value judgments, the problem with existentialism is that it is morally neutral. A leap of faith towards Hitler is no less valid than a leap of faith away from him."[5] The existentialists themselves said as much. Jean-Paul Sartre was a defiant resister of fascism in occupied France. But when a student asked for advice, whether he should risk his life with the

Resistance or stay home with his mother, Sartre told him, "You are free, therefore choose—that is to say, invent. No rule of general morality can show you what you ought to do."[6] Such a decision is up to the individual, who alone bears responsibility for his actions. There are no universal moral values to make up his mind for him. To evade responsibility by refusing to make the decision for oneself is to act in "bad faith."

For Sartre, even ostensibly evil actions could be moral if they were performed in "good faith." In his book *St. Genet*, Sartre celebrates the life of a criminal. Jean Genet was a robber, a drug dealer, a sexual deviant. By all conventional standards, he was an evil man. But Sartre argued that Genet was in fact morally exemplary. Genet consciously chose to do what he did. He took full responsibility for his actions. By refusing to succumb to society's norms and by foregoing all excuses that society was to blame for his actions, Genet exerted his will and lived up to his own self-chosen values. He acted in "good faith." Existentially, he was a saint.[7]

Sartre believed that an authentic existence was not only self-chosen, but "engaged." Choosing a meaning involves making a commitment. Once the choice has been made, one's innate freedom is surrendered to the external demands of the cause. Sartre chose Marxism as the cause of his life, even though Marxist determinism flies in the face of all of his philosophical assumptions. Not only was Sartre a Marxist, he went so far as to call himself a Maoist.[8] It is surely significant that Sartre's moral philosophy, despite his resistance to fascism, led him to embrace another totalitarian ideology.

That philosophers who stress a radical freedom of the will should commit themselves to authoritarian political ideologies is surely a paradox. But elements within existentialism itself make this possible.

There are two sides to the coin of existentialism. While human consciousness is free, the physical and social realms are not. Existentialism tends to accept a deterministic view of the external world, which follows the iron laws of scientific causality. The objective world is absurd precisely because its dead orderliness has so little connection with human consciousness, which alone is free. Human beings must act on this external world, creating meaning by imposing their will on an absurd universe. Nietzsche stresses the individual will, but sees nature and ultimately human life itself to be locked into the causality of eternal return.[9] Thus, existentialists have no problem in accepting deterministic accounts of nature or of society. Sartre's analyses of society and the human condition draw heavily upon the deterministic methodologies of Marx and Freud.

Once the free commitment is made and the consciousness becomes engaged in the external world, freedom becomes self-limiting. Engagement involves immersing oneself in life, with all of its absurdities and intractable determinism. Choosing a meaning involves submitting to the logic of the ideology one has chosen. To repeat Heidegger's words, "To give oneself the law is the highest freedom." But the law once given, once chosen, must be obeyed.

Similarly, existentialism speaks not only of those who are *authentic,* who act in *good faith.* The other side of the coin is its view of those who are "inauthentic," who act in "bad faith." Sartre believed that most people do not want "the burden of freedom." Instead of choosing their own destiny, the masses are content to have someone else—the church, the state, their neighbors—make their decisions for them. The inauthentic masses do follow blindly, purposefully rejecting their freedom. They succumb to the determinisms of the external world. Only the few—the intellectual, the artist, the outcast—dare face the absurdity of life and have the courage to exercise genuine existential freedom.

Nietzsche divides the human race into those who command and those who are commanded. "He who cannot obey himself is commanded." In other words, those who are incapable of creating their own values must obey others. Nietzsche believes that "commanding is harder than obeying; and not only because he who commands must carry the burden of all who obey." Commanding involves "hazard," because the commander "must become the judge, the avenger, and the victim of its own law." But even the commanded, Nietzsche concludes, surrender their freedom because they choose to do so: "That the weaker should serve the stronger, to that it is persuaded by its own will."[10]

For all of his emphasis upon the will, Nietzsche can still write about *The Error of Free Will* (the title of one of his sections in *Twilight of the Idols*). Morally, there is no such thing as free will. "The doctrine of the will has been invented essentially for the purpose of punishment, that is, because one wanted to impute guilt." Because there is no purpose in existence, no morality, and no God, there is no moral responsibility. Reasoning backwards, there is no free will. There is only the whole:

> One belongs to the whole, one is in the whole; there is nothing which could judge, measure, compare, or sentence our being, for that would mean judging, measuring, comparing, or sentencing the whole. But there is nothing besides the whole. That nobody is held responsible any longer . . . that alone is the great liberation. . . . We deny God, we deny the responsibility in God: only thereby do we redeem the world.[11]

For Nietzsche, the individual becomes part of the vast organic unity of the cosmos. Nothing transcends this unity. There is no guilt because there is no one to judge and nothing to judge by. The release that comes from losing oneself in the whole, and thus having no free will or responsibility, is experienced as a liberation. This immanent, secular spirituality removes guilt not by the forgiveness of sins, but by denying morality; the world is redeemed, not by the self-sacrifice of God, but by the human act of denying God.

The tortuous lines of thinking by which a philosophy of radical freedom metamorphoses into an absolute dictatorship may not be logically tenable. And yet, the psychology is clear. The individual makes a choice, and then is bound to what is chosen. The individual will asserts itself over against other wills, and thus must suppress them to rule over them. Existentialism has an elitist strain, with the self-aware, self-determining existential hero set against the inauthentic, conforming masses. Thinking along these lines can lead the existential hero into assuming, like Nietzsche, that because he has created his own values, he is worthy of commanding those who can only obey. The existential concepts of the common will, the community, and the whole give further bases for constructing a totalized worldview. Whereas other partisans of the same ideology may assume that the totalized worldview is objectively true, existentialists recognize it as being constructed; but since they did the constructing, by their own authentic wills, the ideology becomes all the more worth following and worth imposing upon others.

Existentialism on the individual level is good at saying no. As such, it promotes resistance to all external authority. In this sense, it can be a brake against fascism. But the moment the existentialist says yes to something—that is, imposes the inner will onto the external world—the choice must be arbitrary and thus risks being tyrannical. When existentialism takes on a collective, rather than an individualistic, identity and when it takes on the project of molding society and the world, tyranny is inevitable. If there are no transcendent absolutes, ethical action becomes a matter of one will being imposed upon other wills. Since there are no universal reference points, rational discussion, persuasion, and consensus are pointless. All that remains is the sheer exercise of power.

When the existential will goes so far as to be translated into laws, those laws must be coercive, since the validity of all higher authority has been denied. During Hitler's regime, the Academy of German Law sponsored a conference on the philosophy of law. Its purpose was to find ways of replacing objective legal conceptions (as enshrined in both the classical and the Hebraic tradition, in Roman law and in the "Jewish" Bible) with a new organic German law. Heidegger was a participant in the conference, as was Alfred Rosenberg, the race theorist and Nazi ideologue. Rosenberg succinctly summarized existential ethical theory as adopted by the Nazis: "Justice is what the Aryan man deems just. Unjust is what he so deems."[12]

He does not say that justice is what benefits the state or what advances the Aryan race. That would be to remain in the realm of objectivist ethics. Rather, justice and injustice have no other ground than the *fiat* of the Aryan man. Rosenberg's is an existential ethic.

This is not to say that all existentialism leads to fascism. Existentialism perhaps manifests itself most purely in resistance to all authority. But the paradoxes of existentialism are mirrored by the paradoxes of fascism. Scholars have noted a critical distinction between fascism in opposition and fascism in power.[13] Fascism begins in a revolutionary mode, which attacks the status quo. In this phase, fascists are iconoclastic and permissive, attacking all established authority, advocating sexual freedom, and promoting radical artistic and cultural experimentation. When the fascists gain power, however, they must defend the new status quo that they have created. The questioning of all authorities gives way to the elevation of a new authority that must not be questioned. Permissiveness gives way to suppression. Subversion of order is replaced by the construction of a new order. Ernst Röhm and, to a lesser extent, Heidegger, were caught unaware in this shift, when Hitler decided to purge his radicals. But the negations of existentialism were critical in the fascist project of dismantling the transcendent ethic of the Judeo-Christian tradition. Still aided by existential theory, the fascists went on to construct a new ethic of their own.

Organic Ethics

David Hirsch, in his study of Holocaust literature, concludes that one of the most striking characteristics of those who carried out the exterminations was their inability to have empathy with an "other."[14] Hans Ebeling criticizes Heidegger in similar terms: "the power of acknowledging the other as the other, as essentially equal, is missing, and for that reason it only remains to oppress the other without any leniency."[15] Since existentialism focuses upon the individual consciousness, "the other" is necessarily minimized.

The attempt to forge a new ethic based on immanence rather than transcendence was a conscious project of fascist theorists. The French proto-fascist George Sorel sought to establish a morality based not on abstract concepts, but in states of the soul and in consciousness.[16] His book *Reflections on Violence* urges revolt against bourgeois morality and bourgeois political values, including the notion of natural rights and democracy.[17] Sorel was an "irrationalist," urging that the alienating abstractions of reason and morality be replaced by the unleashing of human emotions. This leads Sorel to preach the virtues of violence. "As an alternative to the product of European rationalism," says Sternhell of Sorel and his colleagues, "they offered the cult of feeling, emotion, and violence."[18]

The theorists of fascism understood that the new morality would have to be very different from the old. Heidegger makes a sharp distinction between the values of National Socialism and those of Christianity and humanism when he predicts "a tough struggle to the end in the spirit of National Socialism, which will not be drowned by Christian and humanist notions."[19]

Thus, violence could be turned into a positive moral value, even though (and perhaps because) this completely inverts both Christian and humanistic teachings. Fascist theorists also adopted Nietzsche's critique of compassion. Ezra Pound wrote a poem on the subject, in which Artemis, the goddess of the hunt, laments the rise of Pity:

Compleynt, compleynt I heard upon a day,
Artemis singing, Artemis, Artemis
Agaynst Pity lifted her wail:
Pity causeth the forests to fail,
Pity slayeth my nymphs,
Pity spareth so many an evil thing.
Pity befouleth April,
Pity is the root and the spring.
Now if no fayre creature followeth me
It is on account of Pity,
It is on account that Pity forbideth them slaye.[20]

The sentiment is the same as Nietzsche's:

> We are deprived of strength when we feel pity.... Pity makes
> suffering contagious.... Pity crosses the law of development,
> which is the law of *selection*. It preserves what is ripe for destruc-
> tion; it defends those who have been disinherited and condemned
> by life; and by the abundance of the failures of all kinds which it
> keeps alive, it gives life itself a gloomy and questionable aspect.[21]

Compassion is a kind of sentimentality that violates the laws of
nature, in which the strong thrive and the weak die out.

Fascism advocated a new organic ethic, which would affirm
death as a natural part of life. The Judeo-Christian ethic of love and
compassion has led only to corruption and decay. Death is seen as
a great evil to be avoided at all cost. In nature, though, death is
casual—it happens with every meal. Death is essential to the health
of the species, as weaker specimens are winnowed out and as car-
nivores feed on their prey. The Judeo-Christian position, that death
is an enemy, keeps the weak alive, draining the resources of the
healthy. The supposed benevolence of helping the poor, the mentally ill, and the unsuccessful actually preserves these maladies and
allows them to flourish, thereby weakening the whole society.

Judeo-Christian ethics only prolong suffering. The result is social
decay and emotional corruption. As Pound puts it, "Nothing is now
clean slayne/But rotteth away."[22] The callousness towards human life
exhibited in the death camps may have partially been due to this
shift in the moral imagination. Death was not seen to be so bad.
Therefore, neither was killing.

This organic, back-to-nature ethic had contradictory implications for sexuality. Some fascists advocated sexual freedom, the untrammeled "natural" expression of sexual desires. Their moral reform struck at the restrictions and taboos of traditional morality. Others, just as consistently, argued that sex in nature exists for the reproduction of the species. Their moral reform was along the lines of eugenics, of selective breeding to improve the race. This meant, in practice, restrictions on sexuality, which sometimes resembled the old moral order but with a very different rationale. The difficulty and contradictions involved in formulating an organic sexual ethic—which *is* natural sexuality?—was one of the factors in the great ideological schism within the National Socialist Party that led to the purge of Röhm and his Storm Troopers.

Italian and French fascism always stressed sexual freedom. The German movement was more conservative, but before it assumed power, assaults on "bourgeois" sexual values and sexual repression were common.[23] National Socialism, an uneasy alliance of both continental fascism and biological ideology, had also to come to terms with homosexuality.

World War I veterans had become the backbone of the National Socialist movement as a broadly-based political organization. The experience of combat—with its thrills, dangers, and heroism—was idealized. Groups of veterans met together to keep alive their wartime camaraderie and to lament the betrayal of the Treaty of Versailles. These veterans' groups grew more and more militant and, once they were introduced to National Socialism, would form the cadres of Röhm's SA. In their brown-shirted uniforms, these Storm Troopers would violently disrupt rival political rallies, initiate pogroms against Jews, commit acts of terrorism, and, in general, brutalize or kill any enemies of National Socialism. They were the shock troops of the fascist revolution in Germany.

These paramilitary cells developed a distinctly masculinist mystique. The concept of *Männerbund*, the bond of men, became an essential part of SA ideology. This was part machismo, celebrating the "manly" virtues of fighting and strength. Perhaps more importantly, it emphasized the comradeship of the trenches, the intimacy of men who risk danger together and who are willing to die for each other. This idealization of male friendship often led to homosexual behavior. The more conservative elements of German society and of the Nazi party were scandalized that the SA was rife with homosexuality. This was most evident in the flagrant lifestyle of its leader, Ernst Röhm.[24]

For the biological theorists of the party, such as Rosenberg, the organic function of sex was to breed the Aryan race. Hitler, while he said that what Röhm did in private was his own business, agreed with this eugenic, functional view of sexuality.[25] In this view, promiscuity is dangerous—not because it violates a transcendent moral law—but because it leads to indiscriminate breeding. Homosexuality is wrong—again, not because of some objective moral principle—but because it twists sex away from its biological and racial function.

On the "Night of the Long Knives," the SS burst into the bedrooms of the leading SA officers and killed both them and their male lovers. This initiated a wholesale persecution of homosexuals. They were rounded up and shipped to the concentration camps, where many of them were killed. National Socialism went from openness to and even cultivation of homoeroticism to brutal repression. Psychologists have offered explanations for this shift,[26] but the persecution of homosexuals had a distinct ideological dimension. Homosexual behavior was associated with Röhm and the disruptive cultural radicalism which his faction of the party embodied. Only after Röhm and the SA were purged did persecution of homosexuals begin.[27]

The decision to purge Röhm meant an official commitment to biological and eugenic ideology, including its more restrictive view of sexuality. Nevertheless, the masculinist flavor of the Third Reich remained. "Manly" virtues were everywhere extolled, and depictions of naked men adorned government offices. Women were sometimes idealized as the spiritual inspiration of German manhood and sometimes reduced to breeding stock. Although Nazi women's groups pressed for the rights of women, on the whole, women were firmly subordinated to men.[28]

After the Röhm purge, sexual values under National Socialism were still very different from Judeo-Christian morality. While the regime was ostensibly committed to "family values" as construed by the eugenicists, the biological imperative overrode the values of traditional morality. Bearing children for the state and the war effort was more important than the bonds of matrimony. Party propaganda honored the unwed mother. Himmler said that German women and girls of good blood could serve the fatherland by bearing children even apart from marriage. Special homes and subsidies for unwed mothers were set up for this purpose, and the illegitimate children of SS members were promised special pensions.[29] Prostitution was also accepted. Special plans were made to replenish the population once the war would be over. Martin Bormann said that after the war, "pursuant to special application, men shall be permitted to enter permanent marriage bonds not only with one woman, but with one additional woman."[30]

Abortion was promoted and indeed forced upon "alien" women such as Poles and Slavs in prison camps and in occupied territories.[31] To keep up the supply of children, abortion was prohibited for Aryan women. Sterilization courts, however, could permit abortions in the case of a "racial emergency," that is, when there was evidence of "mixed blood" or birth defects.[32]

The Nazis' organic ethics can perhaps best be summarized by Hitler:

> While Nature, by making procreation free, yet submitting survival to a hard trial, chooses from an excess number of individuals the best as worthy of living, thus preserving them alone and in them conserving their species, man limits procreation, but is hysterically concerned that once a being is born it should be preserved at any price.[33]

He, of course, proposes following nature's way, in which procreation is free, but the weak die out. There is a hint of the early Nazi libertinism, although procreation would not be quite so free once the eugenics program was fully in place. But here is the eugenic rationale, the romantic affirmation of nature, the critique of compassion, and the acceptance of death. With the Judeo-Christian ethic thoroughly discredited and indeed turned upside down, the moral justification for the Holocaust was in place.

Toward the Holocaust

Eugenics, the attempt to improve society by the selective breeding of human beings, enjoyed wide intellectual respect in the late 19th and early 20th centuries. The leader of the eugenics movement in England was Karl Pearson, described as "a social Darwinist who developed into an imperialist, a nationalist, and a racist."[34] George Bernard Shaw, a devoté of Nietzsche who flirted with other proto-fascist ideas, was a member of Pearson's circle. He agreed with Pearson that "nothing but a eugenic religion can save our civilization from the fate that has overtaken all previous civilizations."[35] So did H. G. Wells, who advocated "the sterilization of failures."[36]

Proponents of sexual liberation made common cause with the eugenics movement. The free-sex pioneer Havelock Ellis was a member of Pearson's movement and later defended Hitler's eugenics program.[37] The birth-control movement was also an outgrowth of eugenic theories.

Margaret Sanger, the founder of Planned Parenthood, summarized her goals accordingly: "More children from the fit, less from the unfit—*that* is the chief aim of birth control."[38] Among the unfit, Sanger included those with mental problems, the handicapped, and poor people generally. Assuming that social problems are the result of biological determinism, she believed that crime and poverty can be eliminated simply by sterilizing the poorer classes. Eugenics often merged with racism. Sanger sought to stop the population growth of blacks, Jews, Southern Europeans (such was her American antipathy to newly-arriving immigrants) and, in short, "all non-aryan people."[39] In her book *Pivot of Civilization*, Sanger wrote,

> The philanthropists who give free maternity care encourage the healthier and more normal sections of the world to shoulder the burden of unthinking and indiscriminate fecundity of others; which brings with it, as I think the reader must agree, a dead weight of human waste. Instead of decreasing and aiming to eliminate the stocks that are most detrimental to the future race of the world, it tends to render them to a menacing degree dominant.[40]

Sanger became extremely interested in National Socialism and its eugenics program. A Nazi propaganda tract, *The Rising Tide of Color Against White World Supremacy*, was favorably reviewed in the *Birth Control Review* (October 1920). Lothrop Stoddard, board member of Sanger's American Birth Control League, interviewed Hitler and was impressed by his ideas. Margaret Sanger invited Eugen Fischer, Hitler's advisor on race hygiene, for a speaking engagement in the United States. Ernst Rudin, Hitler's director of genetic sterilization and one of the founders of the Society for Racial

Hygiene, published an article entitled "Eugenic Sterilization: An Urgent Need," in a special eugenics issue of *Birth Control Review* (April 1953).[41]

The feeling was not completely mutual—Sanger's emphasis upon birth control fell afoul of the wartime efforts to increase the German birthrate, and her works became banned.[42] The point is, eugenics and the racial and biological theories that supported it, were often advocated by progressive, reform-minded intellectuals. Eugenic schemes were in the air. The distinction of the Nazis was that they put into practice what many people were thinking about.

The Nazi regime practiced both positive and negative eugenics. The former involved promoting marriages and offspring in those of "good blood." One requirement for membership in the SS was Aryan racial features, which were carefully recorded and studied. Marriages of SS members had to be approved, to be sure that the couple had desirable genetic and racial characteristics. Himmler's eugenic experiments with the SS involved subsidies to those with "racially valuable" children. A more sinister policy was the kidnapping of "biologically valuable" children—those of Aryan heritage or characteristics—in the occupied countries.[43]

Negative eugenics meant eliminating undesirable genetic strains. The sterilization law required that the mentally ill and those with hereditary diseases be surgically sterilized. Physicians were required to report those to whom the law would apply. With the cooperation of health institutions and the medical profession, supported by police power, the law was carried out. Between 200,000 and 350,000 were sterilized.[44] In August 1933, the Bavarian commissioner of health made a speech in which he argued that sterilization was insufficient. The mentally ill, he argued, should be euthanized.[45]

Euthanasia was also in the air. In 1920, Karl Binding and Alfred Hoche published a treatise entitled *The Permission to Destroy Life Unworthy of Life*. It outlined a legal rationale for allowing "death assistance" on the part of physicians, for the "killing of the consenting participant." Those who suffered brain damage or mental retardation were already in a state of "mental death." In a sense, they are already dead. Seriously ill patients should be allowed to give their consent to euthanasia. In the case of those mentally unable to consent, a three-person panel could make the decision. The book emphasized the economic burden on society of keeping the hope-lessly ill and institutionalized alive. It argued that euthanasia was compassionate and consistent with medical ethics, "purely a healing treatment."[46]

The book was a popular success, going through two editions in two years, and it was enormously influential.[47] Its arguments were essentially the same as those of books on the subject today. The authors' concept of "life unworthy of life" could be easily expanded.

Popular acceptance of euthanasia was cemented by a movie entitled *I Accuse*. It was about a physician with an incurably ill wife, who pleads with him to end her suffering. Out of his great love for her, he gives her a lethal injection. The plot, the thematic bias, and the emotional manipulation are reminiscent of contemporary made-for-TV movies on the subject. *I Accuse* was made at the suggestion of Karl Brandt, head of the Nazi euthanasia project. The film was designed to test public opinion about the subject, to see to what extent the public could accept euthanasia. Screening of the film was followed by careful polling of the viewers. The data revealed that most people, including doctors, believed that the husband did the right thing in killing his wife.[48]

The first official legalized "mercy killing" was the result of an emotional case brought before the Führer himself. A baby named Knauer was born blind, missing a leg and part of a hand, and evi-dently mentally retarded. The father begged permission for the child to be put out of his misery. Hitler investigated and granted per-mission. More petitions followed.

An official policy was drawn up, creating an active program to euthanize infants. Midwives and doctors were required to report all cases of babies born with mental handicaps or other birth defects. A medical panel was established which, on the basis of a detailed questionnaire, decided whether "treatment"—that is, euthanasia—should be carried out. Older children suffering from birth-related handicaps were soon drawn into the program. By 1940, 30 centers had been set up for the killing of children.[49]

On September 1, 1939, Hitler wrote a letter authorizing "that patients whose illness, according to the most critical application of human judgment, is incurable, can be granted release by euthana-sia."[50] As Fredric Wertham points out, "the note does not give the order to kill, but the *power* to kill."[51] The decision was up to the doctors.

A program known only as "T4" was set up which applied the procedures set up for euthanizing children to adults. Psychiatrists and physicians were required to fill out questionnaires about their patients. The forms were forwarded to an expert panel, which decided which patients should be euthanized. Patients in mental hospitals, long-term care facilities, and nursing homes were the main targets. In 1939, there were over 300,000 patients in mental hospitals. In 1940, there were only 40,000. At least 275,000 mental patients of all ages were killed. Elderly people plagued with senility were euthanized. Many of the aged and infirm in nursing homes were killed. Euthanasia was then extended to those with merely physical, non-genetic handicaps. The next victims were the crippled (including those who lost a limb in World War I) and the deaf. Attention was next turned to behavioral problems: social misfits and children in reform schools were eliminated.[52]

Despite their openness to the idea after watching *I Accuse,* when German citizens realized that their parents, grandparents, and children were being killed, they were aghast. Individuals boldly flooded government offices with protests. The churches were particularly vocal in their opposition. The Confessional and Catholic Churches spoke out openly and prophetically against these killings. They rejected the concept of "life unworthy of life" and insisted on the Judeo-Christian principle that human beings are created in the image of God, and that therefore each life is objectively valuable.

Hospital chaplains were especially active in defending their flocks. One of them, Pastor Paul-Gerhard Braune, wrote a powerful document addressed to Hitler himself which refuted the moral arguments for euthanasia and forcefully attacked medicalized killing. "Whom if not the helpless," he wrote, "should the law protect?" Pastor Braune was arrested by the Gestapo and imprisoned, but his paper was widely circulated and had its effect.[53]

The Catholic Bishop of Münster, Clemens Count von Galen, condemned the euthanasia program from the pulpit, invoking the wrath of God on those who killed the innocent. Copies of his sermon circulated throughout Germany and helped change the climate of public opinion.[54] Even the pro-Nazi *German Christians* came to oppose the euthanasia program.[55]

In response to the public outcry, the T4 program was officially cancelled in 1941, although killings continued in secret.[56] The medical euthanasia program, however, provided the expertise and the experience for an even more ambitious project. Once euthanasia had become institutionalized and practiced on a large scale, special techniques and facilities were developed. At first, when medical killing was practiced on only a small scale, patients were killed by lethal injection, or sometimes starvation. The killing technology grew more sophisticated and efficient, able to accommodate large numbers of patients at once. After much research and engineering ingenuity, the gas chamber was invented.

Euthanasia facilities were installed in the concentration camps, the large compounds for the imprisonment and forced labor of enemies of the Reich—particularly the Jews. Those who were weak, sick, or otherwise unable to work, were "euthanized."[57]

It had become legitimate to kill "life unworthy of life." And, according to National Socialism, the phrase surely applied to the Jews. Throughout the occupied territories as well as Germany, Jews were rounded up and deported to the camps. The decision was made to exterminate them all. The techniques, the facilities, and—most importantly—the moral inversion of the Judeo-Christian ethic were all in place for the "final solution."

7

"The Beautiful Ideas Which Kill"
Fascism and Modernism

And whoever must be a creator in good and evil, verily, he must first be an annihilator and break values. Thus the highest evil belongs to the highest goodness: but this is creative.

—Nietzsche[1]

Nothing makes me more certain of the victory of our ideas than our success in the universities.

—Adolf Hitler (1930)[2]

Fascism became a mass movement, but it had its origins among intellectuals and artists. In the beginnings of the 20th century, they felt most acutely the alienation that bred fascism. Anson Rabinbach has said that intellectuals turned to fascism because "they had a sense of malaise, of having been defeated by history."[3] Alastair Hamilton offers another explanation: "Fascism, the Fascism of the intellectuals above all, had its origins in sheer rebelliousness, in an anarchistic revolt directed against the established order."[4] This combination of malaise and rebellion, in the context of the intellectual currents described in chapter 2, made the practical program of fascism seem compelling. Fascism seemed to offer cultural renewal. For awhile at least, fascism was avant-garde.

The *modernist* movement in literature and the arts in many ways paralleled and overlapped with the rise of fascism. The modernists believed that the old civilization and its artistic styles were irrelevant after the catastrophe of World War I. New ways of writing and making art must be developed that would be fitting to express the realities of the 20th century. This desire to employ modern styles was, iron-

113

ically, coupled with a revulsion against modern society itself. The modernists almost universally portrayed the modern world as bleak, shallow, and fragmented. In their reaction against their own time, they idealized past civilizations—Pound's Renaissance Italy; Hulme's Middle Ages; D. H. Lawrence's Aztecs—and sought to restore a mythic consciousness. Modernism thus combined stylistic radicalism and social iconoclasm with reactionary or primitivistic cultural ideals.

Fascism, likewise emerging in the disenchantment that followed World War I, purported to be both radically new and radically old. Fascists, like the modernists, castigated the existing civilization and proposed revolutionary new structures and values that had resonances deep in the past. The two movements are more than parallel. That many, if not most, of the modernists, at least for a time, identified themselves with fascism is one of the best kept secrets of literary history.

To be sure, many who flirted with fascist ideology repudiated it, once the atrocities of Hitler's regime became clear. We now have the benefit of hindsight. Perhaps the cultural leaders who embraced fascism should be excused for their naiveté, for being taken in, like so many others, by propaganda and deceit. As Hamilton has observed,

> The consequences of Hitler's ideas, the victims of persecution and discrimination, the disgrace incurred by Mussolini . . . tend to obscure the atmosphere in which fascism developed and to becloud that period when hardly anyone imagined to what it could lead. . . . Writers, known for their hatred of democracy, had little reason to believe that their apologies for violence would go farther than the paper on which they expressed them.[5]

In other words, it is one thing to play with ideas, and another to see them enacted.

It can also be argued that the distinguished thinkers whose ideas were taken over by the fascists were taken out of context and misunderstood. They should not be held responsible for the way their sophisticated ideas were distorted and misused by ignorant and corrupt politicians. Nevertheless, as Zeev Sternhell argues, the intellectuals cannot avoid responsibility for the impact of their ideas upon those who took them seriously:

> Though philosophers and scientists cannot be held responsible
> for the uses made of their teachings, for the way they are inter-
> preted and the meaning read into their thoughts, it was never-
> theless their teachings which, when put into the hands of a
> thousand minor intellectuals who frequently had little aptitude
> for careful philosophical reasoning, shaped a new intellectual cli-
> mate. In the aftermath of the dreadful shock of the war, the Soviet
> revolution, and the economic crisis, that intellectual climate al-
> lowed fascism to burgeon and grow into a powerful mass move-
> ment. For the masses were by then well conditioned to accept a
> new interpretation of the world and of human realities, and even
> a new morality, as the foundation of a new order.[6]

Those who attacked democracy, ridiculed morality, and celebrated
violence may have done so in highly sophisticated ways, but it is
hardly surprising that some of their readers took them literally and
became antidemocratic, immoral, and violent.

The artists and intellectuals helped to shape and were shaped
by the spirit of their age. Modris Eksteins goes so far as to argue
that "Nazism was a popular variant of many of the impulses of the
avant-garde. It expressed on a more popular level many of the same
tendencies and posited many of the same solutions that the avant-
garde did on the level of 'high art.' "[7]

The influence of the modernists on 20th-century art and culture
has been profound, and it continues. The elements in their work
that once aligned them with fascism are part of their continuing
influence.

Modernists and Fascism

A key moment in the birth of modernism was the performance
on May 29, 1913, of Igor Stravinsky's ballet *The Rites of Spring*.
Instead of the lush music and graceful, stylized gesture of traditional
ballet, this music was atonal and harsh. The dancers moved in a
ritualistic, but passionate way, spinning and thrashing. *The Rites of
Spring* portrayed primitive people, at one with nature, celebrating
the coming of spring. The celebration culminated in human
sacrifice.[8]

Shocked by the brutality of both the music and the theme, the
audience at that first performance rioted. *The Rites of Spring* was

hailed, however, as an icon by the avant-garde, particularly after World War I. As Modris Eksteins observes,

> The ballet contains and illustrates many of the essential features for the modern revolt: the overt hostility to inherited form; the fascination with primitivism and indeed with anything that contradicts the notion of civilization; the emphasis on vitalism as opposed to rationalism; the perception of existence as continuous flux and a series of relations, not as constants and absolutes; the psychological introspection accompanying the rebellion against social convention.[9]

Such art was both radically new and radically primitive. In its organicism, its evocation of a mythical consciousness, and its rejection of sentimentality and conventional morality, *The Rites of Spring* can serve as a paradigm for both the modernist movement and the fascist imagination.

The pivotal figure of modernism, who knew and influenced nearly every major author of his day, was Ezra Pound, who devoted his life and his career to fascism. Pound's attack on "abstraction," for which he held the Jews responsible, lies behind his own poetic program of imagism. As a corollary of his own fascist rejection of transcendence, Pound insisted that poems should consist of tangible, concrete images.[10]

Pound became associated with an artistic movement in England known as the Vorticists. Influenced by the proto-fascist Italian Futurists, the Vorticists likewise rebelled against traditional values and championed an art based not on static ideals but on dynamic energy.[11] One member of this circle was T. E. Hulme, a poet and critic who collaborated with Pound in beginning the Imagist movement. Hulme was antihumanist and a defender of militarism. Unlike Pound, however, he did not completely reject Christianity, basing his particular cynicism on the doctrine of original sin. Perhaps the major Vorticist was the artist and writer Wyndham Lewis. Although he would change his opinions with the war, he wrote a number of books and articles promoting fascism and defending Hitler.[12]

Hulme and Pound, as well as T. S. Eliot, were influenced by the classicism and formalism of the early fascist thinker Charles Maurras.[13] France, perhaps as much as Germany or Italy, was a hotbed of activity for the early fascist avant-garde. Besides Maurras, novelists such as Céline and Blanchot combined innovative stylistic experimentation with violence and anti-Semitism. George Sorel contributed to the main stream of literary modernism when he explored in *Reflections on Violence* the power of images and of myth.[14]

W. B. Yeats flirted with fascism in his involvement with Irish nationalism. He wrote songs for the "Blue Shirts," an Irish fascist organization, and at one point spoke highly of Hitler and Mussolini.[15] His own synthesis of myth, primitivism, and nationalism had affinities to fascism. Yeats's idiosyncratic theory of history, in which one phase of civilization would be followed by its opposite, seemed to predict that a rationalistic, moralistic democracy would be followed by its opposite, an emotional, brutal dictatorship.[16]

Shaw, with his vitalistic philosophy and enthusiasm for eugenics, praised Mussolini as a fellow socialist and critic of democracy.[17] The South African-born poet Roy Campbell attacked democracy and defended violence and slavery.[18] D. H. Lawrence, particularly in his novels *Aaron's Rod* and *The Plumed Serpent*, expressed his sympathy for Italian fascism, which paralleled his own primitivism and naturalism.[19] Another key figure in literary modernism was the Norwegian novelist and Nobel-prize-winner Knut Hamsun, who openly supported Hitler even during the Nazi occupation of Norway. Another Nobel-prize-winner, Luigi Pirandello, whose plays were not just modernist but anticipated postmodern styles of writing, was a long-time member of the fascist party and had close ties to Mussolini.[20]

The early T. S. Eliot wrote anti-Semitic comments and advocated positions that came very close to fascism. After his conversion to Christianity, as Alistair Hamilton has shown, Eliot's anti-Semitism subsided and his sympathy for fascist causes came to an end. "The fundamental objection to Fascist doctrine," concluded Eliot, "the one which we conceal from ourselves because it might condemn ourselves as well, is that it is pagan."[21] The comment shows an incisive grasp of the real issues. Eliot developed instead a Christian modernism which sought to revivify the Judeo-Christian heritage, rather than choosing, as most of his fellow writers did, to jettison that heritage.[22]

During the War, Ezra Pound became a propagandist for Mussolini, making radio broadcasts to American troops, lecturing them on fascist ideology and urging them to surrender. With the allied victory, Pound was arrested for treason. The American literary and academic establishment rallied to his defense, and instead of standing trial, he was committed to a mental hospital. In 1949, academic critics who had themselves adopted from literary modernism the practice of "new criticism," which insisted upon separating a work of art from its moral significance, awarded him the Bollingen prize. After 12 years in the mental hospital and more pressure from the literary world, Pound was released in 1958. He immediately moved back to Italy. As soon as he arrived in Italy, he raised his right arm in the fascist salute. The gesture was captured on film by a journalist on the scene. The photograph, reproduced as the cover illustration of this book, shows Pound, grinning and unrepentant, still lionized by the intellectual establishment, flaunting his post-war, post-Holocaust fascism.[23]

Most of the other modernists who at first praised fascism changed their tune once their countries went to war with Hitler and the atrocities of fascism became clear. But the rise of modernism and the rise of fascism were clearly interconnected and mutually reinforcing. In the countries where fascism triumphed, the arts developed along explicitly fascist lines, although they would later become caught up in the contradictions of their own ideology.

Fascist Art

Nietzsche, himself a literary genius, presented the artist as a creator, not only of beautiful objects but of values. Cultural change requires artistic change: "Change of values—that is a change of creators," he wrote. Furthermore, this change to new values must involve the breaking of the old values. "Whoever must be a creator always annihilates."[24] The artist must annihilate the old values as a prelude to creating new values and establishing a new cultural order.

Lawrence Lampert, commenting on this and similar passages, summarizes the connection between Nietzsche's view of art and his view of power: "Will to power as truth led to will to power as art, where the greatest art is the founding art that hangs a new tablet of the good over a people."[25]

Underlying everything for Nietzsche is the *will to power*. Knowledge is not the discovery of truth, but the creation of truth, through the imposition of power. Art too—and the values it embodies and

118

communicates—is an imposition of power. Nietzsche means by "tablet of the good" the moral values held by a society, the phrase alluding to the "tablets" of the Ten Commandments. "A table of the good hangs over every people. Behold, it is the tablet of their overcomings; behold, it is the voice of their will to power."[26] Moral principles are not transcendent truths (as in the Judeo-Christian tradition), but expressions of power. Change comes when new tablets are imposed upon the people, and this is done by the artists.

This view exalts the artist as a cultural force. Hamilton describes how Nietzsche's myth of the "artist-tyrants" and of the emerging Superman destroying the old order and giving birth to the new was compelling for artists and intellectuals of the day.[27] The emergence of a mass, democratic society not only threatened to overwhelm the individual, but it threatened to marginalize the artist and intellectual. Fascism offered a "cult of the hero," which empowered the artist and intellectual. Better yet, fascism was also a mass movement, which, unlike democracy with its equality and mediocrity, would be led by the creative elite.[28]

Perhaps no one has explored the psychological allure of fascism, particularly for artists and intellectuals, as profoundly as the German novelist Thomas Mann, who himself flirted with fascism, only to recoil from it and to become one of its most insightful critics. According to Mann, as summarized by D. H. Hirsch, "The artist's desire to escape from bourgeois social bonds has its parallel in the Nazi destruction of conventional norms of good and evil."[29] In his notes for his novel *Doctor Faustus*, Mann describes the artist's

> desire to escape from everything bourgeois, moderate, classical, . . sober, industrious, and dependable into a world of drunken release, a life of bold Dionysiac genius, beyond society, indeed superhuman—above all subjectively, as experience and drunken intensification of the self, regardless of whether the world can go along with it. . . . The bursting of social bonds, which occurs as a disintegration by infectious disease, at the same time *political.* Intellectual-spiritual fascism, throwing off of humane principle, recourse to violence, blood-lust, irrationalism, cruelty, Dionysiac denial of truth and justice, self-abandonment to the instincts and unrestrained "Life," which in fact is *death* and, insofar as it is life, only the *Devil's work.* Fascism [is] . . . a Devil-given departure from bourgeois society that leads through adventures of drunkenly in-

tense subjective feeling and super-greatness to mental collapse and spiritual death, and soon to physical death.[30]

Fascism was a way to throw off the shackles of traditional morality and to experience the thrill of "self-abandonment to the instincts." Mann knew, however, that "unrestrained Life" is in fact death, and that "the drunken intensification of the self" means bondage to the Devil.

In Italy and France, an artistic avant-garde was deeply involved in the formation of fascist ideology.[31] The Italian Futurists are important in art history for the part they played in the development of cubism, for their experiments with dynamic form, and for opening up the art world to the energy and power of modern technology. The *Futurists' Manifesto* also includes what would become the moral values—Nietzsche's "new tablet of the good"—of the new fascist order:

1. We want to sing the love of danger, the habit of energy and rashness.

2. The essential elements of our poetry will be courage, audacity, and revolt.

3. .... We want to exalt movements of aggression, feverish sleeplessness, the forced march, the perilous leap, the slap and the blow with the fist. ...

9. We want to glorify war—the only cure for the world—and militarism, patriotism, the destructive gesture of the anarchists, the beautiful ideas which kill, and contempt for women.

10. We want to demolish museums and libraries, fight morality, feminism, and all opportunist and utilitarian cowardice.[32]

Here is the frenzied, exhilarated release from morality that Mann described. Though clearly designed to shock the bourgeoisie, the *Futurist Manifesto*—in its gleeful celebration of violence and its in-your-face barbarism—was fully realized in Röhm's Storm Troopers. The whole intellectual heritage that led to fascism can be summed up as "The beautiful ideas which kill."

The Futurists' cultivation of violence as a reaction against rationalism is evident in the French author George Valois:

To the bourgeois brandishing his contracts and statistics:

—Two plus three makes. . . .

—Nought, the Barbarian replies, smashing his head in.[33]

Here is a new aesthetic, based not on harmony and warm feelings, but on the release of violence and the giddy thrill that comes from violating taboos.

Mussolini was particularly open to the artistic avant garde, which, in turn, was strongly attracted to Italian fascism. In 1932, one of the most remarkable installations of the century opened in Rome: the Exhibition of the Fascist Revolution (*Mostra della Rivoluzione Fascista*). The *Mostra* was a modernist *tour de force,* a collaboration of Futurist artists, modernist architects, and fascist intellectuals.[34]

At a time when museums consisted mostly of historical objects in display cases, the *Mostra* anticipated contemporary museum design in immersing the visitor in a walk-through multi-media experience. The *Mostra* combined photography, sculpture, music, and graphics, employing the modern art technique of the collage. As viewers would walk through chambers representing the various phases of the fascist revolution, they would be bombarded and overwhelmed by fractured images of war and upheaval, slogans painted on the walls and ceilings, historical artifacts juxtaposed with abstract art. The rooms were characterized by odd angles, ceilings that sometimes dropped and sometimes rose up, abrupt shifts in scale, and other disorienting manipulations of space. As Jeffrey Schnapp describes it, "This constant alteration of the spatial configuration of individual rooms produced a sense of perpetual movement and instability."[35]

One of the nearly 4 million viewers, the fascist poet Ada Negri, describes her impressions of the *Mostra*:

Grandeurs and horrors figured or realized with a representational audacity I never dreamed of: the gigantic statue lives and bears witness alongside the printed and written document, displaying an archive's stamp; paintings, caricatures, photographs are peers with the historical dates and names recalling the heroic battles. Seeming already a legend, the history of those years leaps out at our eyes synchronically and thrusts us into a vortex. There is no defending oneself against its violent assault.[36]

A French art critic, Louis Gillet, reviewed the exhibition, which he described as having been "assembled with all the cuts, welds, ellipses and emphases of a film specialist." He thus recognized the affinity of fascist aesthetics with film (which will be discussed in chapter 9). Relating the exhibit to Futurism, Gillet observed that "everything is calculated according to a unique ballistics so as to machine-gun the spectator, to increase the power to shock."[37]

The fracturing of the objective world and the reconstituting of a humanly-created order, the cultivation of subjectivity and emotionalism in a communal experience, and the attempt to create a new mythic image over against the word are all signs of a fascist art expressing the fascist worldview. In many ways, the *Mostra* went beyond modernism, anticipating the techniques and experimentation of today's contemporary artists: the experiential involvement of the audience, the aesthetics of shock, the multi-media techniques, the breaking of barriers between artistic forms and between art and reality. The *Mostra* was not only modern but postmodern.

Just as Italy had the Futurists, Germany had the Expressionists. Both artistic movements had affinities to fascism. Whereas Italian fascism successfully embraced modern art, German fascism was characteristically more ambivalent, first encouraging and then crushing its artistic avant garde.

German Expressionism—embracing painting, poetry, drama, and film—explored inner psychological states in art of great merit. Violence was a major motif.[38] In rejecting the old values and seeking to forge new ones, some Expressionists turned to Marxism, others to fascism. The German poet Gottfried Benn was one of the latter. As Hamilton describes his project,

> He set out to criticize and destroy rational Western thought since Kant, to sweep away the entire positivist tradition of the nineteenth century.... Benn put all his talent to exploring the decay of his surroundings. He was the first German poet to write about sheer ugliness, to formulate aesthetics of ugliness.[39]

Benn mellowed in his later years, but the "aesthetics of ugliness" permeated all of the arts in the period between the wars. One of the greatest German Expressionist painters was Emil Nolde. Despite his interest in Christianity, Nolde was a racist, a primitivist, and a long-time member of the Nazi party.[40]

Once Hitler assumed power and began to forge the new social order, the role of the artist suddenly changed. The contradictions of fascism—in which the triumph of the will leads to slavery and "unrestrained life" leads to death—once again manifested themselves. Those artists who in many ways shaped the imagination of fascism and helped to bring it to power were turned upon once the power was achieved. Artistic innovation was countered by brutal censorship.

Once again, the turning point in the conflict between the revolutionary spirit and a newly forged cultural conservatism was the purge of Ernst Röhm and the radical faction of the Nazi party. While Goebbels was a patron of avant-garde art, Rosenberg rejected modern art as reflecting Jewish decadence.[41] By opting for a fascism centered in racial theory rather than cultural revolution, Hitler (who himself began as an artist) had little use for cultural revolutionaries once the Third Reich was established. The negativism and iconoclasm that characterized modernist art might be appropriate to reflect and attack the bourgeois order, but it would be subversive to the new folkish community.

The German Expressionists were banned. Gottfried Benn's poetry was censored. Despite his indignant protests, Emil Nolde's paintings were confiscated. Even works by the Italian Futurists were banned. Modernism in the arts was branded "degenerate." A new folkish art was to take its place.

In 1937, the Nazis staged what became the largest art exhibition of the 20th century.[42] In a typically schizophrenic counterpart to the *Mostra*, the Nazis staged a double show, consisting of one exhibition entitled "Degenerate Art" and another entitled the "Great German Art Exhibition." The former consisted of 650 works of modern art, focusing on German Expressionists, but including distinguished modernists from Marc Chagall (attacked because he was a Jew) to the Russian Abstract artist Wassily Kandinsky. The works of Emil Nolde were prominently displayed. The show ridiculed the modern paintings, with labels such as "Revelation of the Jewish racial soul," and "The ideal—cretin and whore."

As Stephanie Barron has observed, the German term translated "degenerate," *entartete*, was "a biological term, defining a plant or animal that has so changed that it no longer belongs to its species."[43] Castigating abstract art for its Jewishness and drawing parallels between the distorted figures of modern art and biological deformity, the show was an attempt to create a racial aesthetic.

123

The companion show, the "Great German Art Exhibition" featured work handpicked by Hitler himself. The new officially sanctioned art featured idealized portraits of Aryan men and women, romantic landscapes that honor the soil of the Fatherland, and nostalgic images of peasant life and folklore.

Nazi art, however, was not bourgeois. The most common subject for the official art seems to have been realistic nudes. Everywhere in Hitler's new Reich Chancellery were paintings and statues of naked women and, especially, naked men. Hitler's favorite sculptor, Arno Breker, said of his nudes that they show the "pure air of instinctive drives." They depict the "revolutionary youth of today, which tears the veil from the body hidden in shame."[44]

These works of art celebrate naturalism and sexual instinct. In their barely suppressed homoeroticism, they recall the *Männerbund* of the early Nazi cells. The realism of the new art reflects the fascist commitment to the concrete, the tangible, as opposed to the transcendent and abstract. National Socialism stressed group identity, as defined by one's race and one's participation in the communal nation, and attacked individualism as a remnant of bourgeois democracy. This is reflected in the statues which, while realistic, portray not distinct individuals but idealized racial models. They are icons of the Aryan body.[45]

Despite the apparent conservatism of style, this new fascist art still reflects the revolutionary ideology. The pseudo-classicism reflects the imposition of order. The landscapes reenforce the cult of the land. The folk art underscores the primitivism that was a major value for the new order. Fascist realism is in fact very similar to socialist realism, the official art of the Soviet Union, which likewise inspired an artistic avant garde only to suppress and censor it once the new socialist order was in place.

Because National Socialism was a popular movement, asserting the unity of all of the German people, it favored popular art. This may be another reason why the often obscure experimentation of the modernists fell out of favor. Art should be accessible to the people. Thus, Nazism encouraged kitsch. The people were bound together by grandiose rituals and mass rallies, which often featured "triumphal processions of kitsch, with huge papier-maché Greek heads borne by people dressed as Rhine Maidens and warriors of the Teutoburg Forest."[46]

124

Fascist art lurched from total freedom to total control. Ultimately, that official Nazi art was so bad was due to its own contradictions, to its stirring up of creativity only to stifle it.[47] Just as it rejected transcendent moral values, fascism denied the basis for transcendent aesthetic values. Both morality and the arts became judged for their social utility, as expressions of the will for power.

The aesthetics of power mean that aesthetic questions become power struggles. Fascism in rejecting the transcendent left no room for objective appraisals or purely aesthetic appreciation. Different art forms are seen as competing constellations of power. A particular style represents a value-creating act of power. Art becomes an act of social aggression. If its values are not those of the common will, it must be countered by another act of power. With such a view of art, censorship and persecution of artists is inevitable. As a result, some good artists became casualties of their own ideology.

The legacy of artistic modernism, while challenged in some ways, still survives. Artists still enjoy defying "bourgeois moral values." Irrationalism is still cultivated. Artists still see themselves as imposing order on a meaningless world. Organicism and new art forms for a new age remain elusive goals. Myth, primitivism, and the unconsciousness are privileged over dogma, civilization, and the intellect. In these senses, fascism still has its influence.

But the fascism that remains in these traces of modernism is a weakened strain. Perhaps it has inoculated Western culture in the postwar years against the more virulent version of the disease. The danger is from the new mutation.

8

"The Will to Power" Fascism and Postmodernism

Purveyors of postmodern ideologies must consider whether it is possible to diminish human beings in theory, without, at the same time, making individual human lives worthless in the real world.

—David H. Hirsch[1]

We . . . seek again to conquer the undestroyed naming power of language and word.

—Martin Heidegger[2]

Today, *modernism* has become old-fashioned. Contemporary thought and contemporary art have assumed a shape of their own. We are in the *postmodern* age. In our eagerness to put the 20th century behind us, we need to notice that the same ideas that coalesced into fascism are making a comeback.

The Judeo-Christian tradition, with its objective morality and transcendent spiritual truth, has been all but erased from the intellectual and cultural establishment. In its place is emerging a new ideology that rejects every kind of intellectual or moral transcendence. In the intellectual world, cultural determinism, the apotheosis of nature, power reductionism, and the critique of all transcendent meaning and values are being reasserted in ever more sophisticated ways. As it turns out, some of the crucial theorists of the new postmodern thought were personally involved with the fascism of the 1930s.

Contemporary Ideology

In the first decades of the 20th century, an existentialist metaphysics stressing the freedom of the will metamorphosed into a

126

political program of oppression and genocide. The intellectual tradition that gave us fascism has continued to develop. The new ideology has gone a long way towards resolving some of the tensions in early fascist theory, such as how to reconcile the triumph of the will with determinism and how to synthesize the individual with culture.

Postmodern ideology can be thought of as a synthesis of Heidegger and Nietzsche with Marx and Freud.[3] The result is a volatile mixture of determinism and libertarianism, quasi-scientific analysis and irrationalism, totalizing worldviews and revolutionary skepticism. There are important intellectual and historical connections between postmodernist ideology and fascism that need to be faced honestly by contemporary theorists.

To be sure, there are some new elements in postmodernism, such as feminism. Postmodernism is not only a development of modernism but a reaction against it (although in a way that seems to heighten the fascist possibilities rather than to minimize them). There are many differences between fascism as a realized political movement and today's intellectual postmodernism. In showing the parallels between postmodernist and fascist theory, I am not accusing postmodernists of being fascists. I only want to call attention to the dangers in certain lines of thinking, showing where they might lead by remembering where they have led before.

Like early fascism, postmodern ideology employs the rhetoric of liberation. The problem in both early fascism and contemporary critical thought is that while the rhetoric sounds progressive and humane, its implications undercut the very possibility of progress and humane values. Postmodern theorists think of themselves as leftist, but their version of Marxism is leavened with philosophical and psychological irrationalism. While they employ a Marxist-style critique of capitalism (as the early fascists also did), their synthesis of social determinism and psychological liberation leads not to some sort of scientifically based socialism but to an organic self-actualizing community—that is, to a national socialism. Postmodern theorists argue that all social relationships are a mask for power; but while they intend their analysis to expose oppression, it could just as easily legitimize oppression by undermining all moral and legal structures that might mitigate and control the "will to power." Postmodernists proclaim the values of pluralism, but in doing so, they have resurrected the old fascist model that mind-sets and personal identity are culturally—or even racially—determined.

Postmodernist thought begins with the existentialist premise that meaning is *created.* Human categories of reasoning and of language impose order on the external world. Scientists find data and imagine a model to account for it; the model in turn shapes the data that will be found. Even a supposedly objective discipline such as science is actually an imposition of the ordering faculties of the human mind. Just as an artist or a novelist create *fictions,* scientists, historians, politicians, and jurists create *fictions* to make sense of their experience and to give order to their disciplines.

Whereas earlier existentialism sees this meaning-making function in the individual will, postmodernism goes on to stress the social dimension of meaning-creation. Impersonal forces of culture, economics, psychology—all mediated by language—shape human behavior. Because meaning patterns are essentially constructions of language, everything becomes a "text." All artifacts of a culture—architecture, clothing, social customs—are signs that embody meaning. They are a kind of language, examples of *texts* that can be read, decoded, and subjected to critical analysis. Such *texts,* like all language, encode the power structures that underlie the society. These power structures are "inscribed" into the minds of every member of that society.

The self is also a *fiction,* or a *text.* Individual autonomy is a myth. We are actually shaped and determined by culture, class, gender, ethnicity, and sexual proclivities—by the whole "language system" that constitutes our consciousness. The experience of being free and autonomous, for example, is illusory, a construction of bourgeois culture with its individualistic values.

Postmodern scholars employ Marxist-style social analysis—explaining phenomena in terms of class struggle, economic injustice, and the conflict between the oppressor and the oppressed. They also employ Freudian categories, accounting for both the individual mind and human culture in terms of Oedipal longings and sexual repression. Uniting both Marx and Freud for postmodern theorists is Nietzsche: Behind both economics and sexuality is the will to power.

According to Marx, Freud, and Nietzsche, reality is masked. Beneath the benign appearances of cultural expressions—from the codes of good manners to the artistry of a novel—is hidden the real meaning of sex, oppression, and power. Postmodern critics seek to uncover what is hidden, to scrutinize and challenge the latent political, sexual, or power messages embedded in the text.

Postmodern critics sometimes speak of "interrogating" a text. The metaphor, calling to mind the practice of the SS or perhaps the KGB, is drawn—no doubt unconsciously—from the police state. The critic takes the role of the secret police. The text is under arrest. The interrogation is designed to ferret out the prisoner's covert political beliefs. The postmodernist critic, like a skillful Gestapo interrogator, might have to use torture, but will assuredly force the text to divulge its politically incorrect secrets.

This approach to scholarship is exemplified by Michel Foucault, whose *Madness and Civilization, Discipline and Punish*, and *History of Sexuality* are provocatively radical analyses of Western history and the human psyche. Foucault interrogates "texts" such as mental hospitals, prisons, the legal system, and all of the cultural artifacts that define them. He presents madness, law, and sexual morality as modes of oppression and tyranny.

In an essay entitled "Nietzsche, Genealogy, History," Foucault, quoting Nietzsche, states that "the concept of liberty is an 'invention of the ruling classes' and not fundamental to man's nature or at the root of his attachment to being and truth."[4] Liberal democracies in effect train individuals to police themselves. Those who think they are free are actually more controlled than those who live in police states. Such a paradoxical analysis not only critiques free societies but legitimizes police states. A democracy is no better than a police state, and a police state is just as good as a democracy. (In fact, it is better because the power is externalized and thus easier to resist.) The concept of individual liberty dissolves. The self is reduced to a plaything of vast, impersonal social forces.

Foucault's sympathies, like those of most postmodern scholars, are always on the side of the oppressed. Unlike Nietzsche's brutal dismissal of the unfit, Foucault takes their side. For Foucault, madness is a social construct, and he champions those who are mad against those who would oppress them by putting them in mental hospitals.[5] He agrees with Nietzsche on the will to power, but unlike Nietzsche his bias is with those who have no power. This may be a brake to a full-blown fascism, but one wonders where the ethical formula comes from and whether it can withstand the force of his own analysis. As Hirsch points out, Foucault

> has always a single goal: to expose the ways in which the so-called ruling class in liberal democracies dominates and oppresses. But while the oppressors are clearly defined by Foucauldian genealogy, it is somewhat more difficult to identify the oppressed. It can't be the individual who is oppressed, because in Foucauldian genealogy "the individual" as a living entity does not exist; the term being nothing more than an expedient construct of the oppressors. Nor can it be a specific class that is oppressed, since in being inscribed by the ideological state apparatus, the dominating class is as oppressed as those it dominates.[6]

Except for Foucault's ungrounded sympathy for the powerless, one wonders where a fascist would disagree with him.

Relativism

Another major tenet of postmodernism is cultural and epistemological relativism. Because meaning is constructed, it varies from person to person. Since meaning is a social construction, different cultures will create different structures of reality. Postmodernists see rationalism and scientific objectivity as themselves manifestations of the Western technological mind, itself historically and culturally conditioned. They reject the "privileging" of these and other distinctly Western modes of knowledge.

Postmodernists tend to criticize Western civilization harshly for its history of oppression and imperialism. For them, the Western heritage is one of racism, sexism, and ethnocentrism. Western culture was built upon the suppression of women and the poor, and the myth of Western superiority has manifested itself in arrogant attempts to dominate other cultures, from the proselytizing of missionaries to colonialism and slavery. Postmodernists reject the pretensions of "Euro-centrism," seeing the history of the world solely from the point of view of Europe. They champion the cause of so-called primitive cultures and those victimized by Western expansionism—native Americans, Africans, Palestinians. Rejecting *Euro-centrism,* some scholars are experimenting with *Afro-centrism.* Postmodernists reject history as written by and about "dead white European males" and write new histories from the point of view of those who have been "marginalized" by the dominant power structures—women, the poor, minorities.

This would seem to be the opposite of what the fascists taught. Fascists glorified the "white European male" culture. They openly scorned the marginalized and powerless, and gleefully and unapologetically oppressed them. Nevertheless, the analysis of Western culture as the history of white dominance over other races is strikingly similar to fascist sociology. The only difference is that what most postmodernist critics decry, the fascists celebrate. They agree on the facts.

In reducing social transactions to issues of raw power, in stressing ethnic rather than individual identity, and in insisting that categories of thought and moral values do not transcend one's culture, the fascists would be in full agreement with the postmodernists. While the postmodernists are trying to uphold the values of tolerance and sympathy for the oppressed, if their picture of the world is correct, such sentiments hardly have a place. If law, morality, art, and civilization are only masks for the exercise of power, then the critic's moral position also must be nothing more than a power statement. If the critic and the faction for which the critic has sympathy had power, they would presumably exercise it in an oppressive way like everyone else. If all of the traditional restraints upon power, such as law and morality, are themselves only facades for oppression, why should there be any limits upon what one does with that power? If oppression is the rule of history, why not oppress?

Already race-centric models are emerging that bear ironic resemblance to Alfred Rosenberg's racial reductionism. "The European mind" is supposed to be cold, individualistic, and linear, whereas "The African mind" is warm and communal. "The Eastern mind" is holistic and cyclical. Latin Americans combine European, African, and Native American traits as a result of South American race-mixing. This sort of cultural generalization may have some value, but it risks racial stereotyping. When it hardens into pseudo-scientific categories, as seems to be happening, it risks reviving the old racial sciences.

To be sure, whereas the old race sciences privileged the white races, the new race sciences privilege the nonwhite. But it matters little which races are affirmed and which races are criticized. Opinions about which is the master race varied. There was a Japanese fascism as well as a German fascism. Practically every ethnic group in Europe, from the Irish to the Croats, had its fascist movements. The centrality of race and ethnicity meant pitting one's own race and ethnic group against all others.

What is missing in postmodern multiculturalism is an acknowledgment of any kind of realm that transcends culture, some overarching sense of universal humanity which people of all cultures have in common. Science, technology, and reason formerly were thought to offer objective truth no matter what culture one comes from. A Chinese scientist could conduct the same experiment and produce the same result as an American scientist. A technological development, such as improved medicine, could save the life of an African woman as well as a British child. Science and technology promised to improve the lives of all people no matter what culture they were born into. Certainly, technology changes culture, and not always for the best. But science and technology, while they created an overarching culture of their own, were in a sense outside of culture. They were, to coin a word in the postmodern style, "metacultural."

Democratic values—human rights, self-governance, personal liberty—were also thought applicable to all cultures. Democracy offered an objectively devised framework that could encompass a variety of cultures, enabling individuals within each culture to participate in the larger society. In doing so, democracy created a culture of its own, with values such as individualism and liberty that sometimes clashed with those of the more organic cultures that composed the society. Still, democracy was thought of as an objective plan that allowed for both unity and diversity, an overarching political structure that could coexist with cultural pluralism. Democracy offered a "metaculture."

Religion, too, was seen as transcendent and not culture-bound. Christianity offered objective moral values that had priority over cultural values. Time-honored cultural practices such as tribal revenge codes and infanticide were changed when the culture embraced Christianity—this applied to the Greeks, Romans, and the Germanic tribes (all of whom practiced personal revenge and infanticide) no less than to Africans and Native Americans. Western Europe had to be evangelized just as New Guinea was evangelized.

Christianity—far from being a "white man's religion" or a "European religion"—was born in the Middle East. Christianity was seen as a Catholic, that is, a universal *metacultural* religion, challenging yet corresponding to the needs of all cultures.

Today, we see these metacultures operating throughout the world. Can we say that science, technology, and capitalism are solely Western in light of the enormous achievements in these fields by Japan, Taiwan, Korea, and other Asian countries? Their technological and economic success can hardly be explained in terms of Western imperialism. These Asian cultures have mastered techniques that they find valuable without erasing their own culture. Democratic revolutions are likewise sweeping the world. Self-government, individual rights, and personal liberty are taken as valuable truths by Africans and Latin Americans who have been chafing for generations under tyrannical governments. Christianity has more vitality in "Third World" countries such as Africa and Latin America than in Western Europe.

An African friend of mine is critical of Western images of Africa, including those of "Afro-centric" intellectuals.[7] Those who glorify the simple tribal life, he says, are keeping his people from getting the technology, the economic growth, and the democratic institutions that they desperately need to improve their lives. His people do not wear shoes, he told me, not because they want to be close to nature but because they are poor. Western, postmodern ideals of "the noble savage" keep his people in their place. Postmodernists would prefer Asians to be mystical and Zenlike, but Asians are now more interested in economic development. Postmodernists, like Western tourists, prefer those of other cultures to dress in their native costumes. But many people in the less-developed countries find their own societies repressive and yearn for the same freedom and prosperity enjoyed by the West. The metacultures of technology, democracy, and a transcendent religion can help them to reform their own cultures. Postmodernist primitivism, they find, is condescending, racist, and antiprogressive.

As John Ellis has observed, "Anyone who thinks that cultural relativism and the celebration of ethnicity must lead to egalitarianism is sadly mistaken: The lesson of history is that they are more likely to unleash dangerous forces of the extreme right."[8] He traces cultural relativism to Herder, the 19th-century German romantic theorist. Herder responded to Germany's alleged inferiority to France by insisting that each culture must be judged in its own terms. No culture is better than another; just different. Herder's writings on culture were important in the rise of German nationalism, which developed, as we know, into National Socialism.[9]

"Our understanding struggles to go beyond the fatal error of believing in the equality of all human beings and tries to recognize the diversity of peoples and races."[10] Such a statement sounds imminently postmodern and politically correct. But it was said by an apologist for fascism. The author of this statement has connections to both fascism and postmodernism: Elfride Heidegger-Petri was Martin Heidegger's wife. Recognizing the diversity of peoples and races for her meant denying the equality and thus the intrinsic worth of all human beings.

Benedetto Croce might be criticizing postmodernism, but he is really attacking the fascism of Heidegger's "Rectoral Address":

> Today, all of a sudden, one falls into the abyss of the falsest historicism, which negates history, which it crudely and materialistically conceives as the assertion of ethnocentrism and racism.[11]

Hirsch has complained that postmodernist concepts such as "the fictionality of history" serve to mask the objective reality of the Holocaust.[12] In fact, revisionist historians are at work trying to interpret it away, trying to construct new models to account for the data, arguing that the extermination of the Jews never happened.[13]

But the Holocaust was objectively real. It was not a meaning-projection onto indeterminate data. It was not merely a "text." The euthanasia clinics and the concentration camps actually existed; the annihilation of six million Jews actually happened. Those who died were not "fictions." What suffered in the camps was not "the myth of the self" but a real person.

Saul Friedlander has pointed out the difficulty of even discussing the Holocaust in terms of contemporary intellectual analysis:

> Any discussion of the "Final Solution" must confront the moral issue. Hence, a problem arises with the application of certain new interpretive strategies. Is it possible to embrace such strategies and yet avoid moral relativism?[14]

Postmodernism, not only in the arcane world of academia but more importantly in popular culture, positively affirms and celebrates

134

moral relativism. If there are no moral absolutes valid for everyone, if morality is either a privately chosen code or the imposition of power over someone else, then "moral issues" dissolve. All actions, including Holocausts, become morally neutral—one person's private opinion against another. And if the unannihilated Jews and the confessional Christians are right, that sin and the proclivity to sin is real, that the bondage of the will means an inexhaustible potential for horrendous evil, then Friedlander's question has a corollary: Is it possible to embrace moral relativism and still avoid another "Final Solution"? The very phrase is a metaphor from a worldview that reduces the world to a text: a "final solution" is the last step of an "interpretive strategy."

Deconstruction

A notable feature of contemporary thought is its preoccupation with theory. Most contemporary theorists would agree with Heidegger, who asserted that "theory is to be understood as the highest realization of true practice."[15] The intellectual heart of postmodern thought is the theory and critical methodology of deconstruction.

The concept of deconstruction has its philosophical roots in Heidegger, who first used the term,[16] although the contemporary theory goes far beyond Heidegger in its dissolution of language and transcendence. Put simply, deconstruction begins with the existentialist dictum that there is *no transcendent meaning,* that *meaning is a human construction.* Deconstructionists go on to show that the way meaning is constructed is through language. Drawing on the work of structural linguists, deconstructionists then argue that language, which is based on arbitrary symbolism and exclusions, is itself problematic. A language construction is unstable, even contradictory. "According to this view," as one critic of the movement explains it, "language is meaningless, in the sense that it subverts its own movement and can never reach beyond itself."[17]

Human beings cannot escape language, which constitutes both the only world that anyone can know and the human mind itself. Yet language is ultimately unstable. Meaning is slippery; interpretations are infinite; no one meaning can be absolute. Texts may seem meaningful, but they contain their own contradiction. The project of deconstruction is to uncover these contradictions, to show the hidden and suppressed meanings that inhere in a text, whether it is a literary work[18] or a social institution. The official meaning of a discourse is determined by power. Postmodern critics "de-con-struct" those meanings, "to read out what is hidden or suppressed in a formulation and thereby to decenter it."[19]

As a critical methodology, deconstruction has been seized upon as a tool of political analysis. Feminist, Marxist, and gay critics can deconstruct novels, television shows, and legal documents by ana-lyzing their language to uncover their oppressive power structures and their inner contradictions. A deconstructionist reading of the Declaration of Independence might interrogate the phrase "all men are created equal." The word "men" excludes women, who in fact were denied legal equality in 1776. The phrase was composed by Thomas Jefferson, a slaveholder. The rhetoric of liberty is contra-dicted by the subtext of sexism and slavery.

In contrast, an analysis grounded in the Judeo-Christian tradition would see the principle of equality as a transcendent moral absolute, grounded in God Himself (the Creator). This moral principle has the status of truth, whether it is followed or not. That Jefferson and the other colonial slaveholders were not consistent with their own ideals does not mean that their ideals were not valid. The bondage of the will makes moral perfection impossible. Yet the ideal of equality, acknowledged here even by slaveholders, initiated the ab-olitionist movement and led eventually to the abolition of slavery. Equality remains elusive, but as long as there is a transcendent and authoritative goal, civil rights movements and other struggles to make the real world comply with the moral absolute become possible.

Deconstructionists would argue that the very word *equality* de-pends for its meaning upon some *inequality* against which the term is defined. *Freedom* means the opposite of *slavery,* so that the pos-sibility of slavery must always be present in order for freedom to be understood. In a truly free and equal society, presumably, there would be no need for such words. Who is free and who is a slave might change in the shifting paradigms of power, but the very rhet-oric of democracy betrays its contradictory foundations.

While the deconstructionist analysis is indeed subversive of the status quo, a political program based on its assumptions could only be antiprogressive and authoritarian. In the Judeo-Christian world-view, progress is possible because there are moral absolutes according to which the world should be reformed. Without a transcendent reference point, there are no criteria for progress. All that is left is the exercise of power. If language is arbitrary, with only a veneer of associations that connect the signifier to the signified, then the exercise of power—whether exercised by democracies, Marxists, feminists, or fascists—must likewise be arbitrary, despite all of the rhetoric with which it justifies itself.

While a deconstructionist methodology can subvert established meanings, there is another corollary. It is impossible to break out of language, for all of its limitations. For deconstructionists, the concept of transcendence, that words point to realities beyond themselves, is the ultimate illusion. Words point only to other words. Language is a prison-house. Words are inadequate, yet they are all we have. To believe in "a transcendental signified," that words point to ideas that themselves have an objective, ontological status, is to be *logocentric*. Logocentrism "identifies language with voice, presence, Western metaphysics, and ultimately derivation from the word of God."[20] The deconstructionist "tries to topple this hierarchy."[21]

Deconstruction, like fascism, is a revolt against transcendence. Its rejection of individual identity, its cultural relativism, its power reductionism, are all sophisticated developments of early fascist theory. But the connections between deconstruction and fascism are more than intellectual parallels and affinities. Although its main theorist, Jacques Derrida, is Jewish, "no fewer than three of the most sterling careers flanking deconstruction," as Jeffrey Mehlman has observed, "were profoundly compromised by an engagement with fascism."[22] Heidegger's fascism has already been discussed. The French novelist and literary theorist Maurice Blanchot, part of Charles Maurras's circle, wrote anti-Semitic articles and calls for terrorism in fascist journals.[23] Paul De Man, who has done more than anyone else to promote deconstruction in the United States, was a Nazi propagandist. To Mehlman's three, we might add a fourth: Hans Robert Jauss, the German receptionist critic (an approach different from but related to deconstruction). He was a member of the Waffen SS.[24]

Paul De Man was a professor at Yale and a key figure in contemporary literary criticism. Shortly after De Man's death in 1984, a researcher seeking to collect his writings discovered that De Man had written over one hundred articles for pro-Nazi periodicals in occupied Belgium. He, of course, kept his background as a fascist journalist secret when he emigrated to the United States and began his academic career. This discovery has profoundly embarrassed the current academic establishment, which thinks of itself as leftist and the polar opposite of any sort of fascism. His defenders insist that De Man abandoned his youthful views and that his deconstruction is a way to cast down all authoritarianism. Others invoke the ad hominem fallacy, saying that De Man's personal failings do not make his intellectual system invalid. Other scholars, especially in light of recent revelations about Heidegger's fascism, are excavating the relationship between fascism and deconstruction.[25]

Paul De Man must have been more than a collaborationist, co-operating with the occupying power out of cowardice or ambition. As has been mentioned, his uncle, Henri De Man, was an important fascist theorist. Henri De Man laid the theoretical foundation for transforming a class-based Marxist socialism to a national socialism. Described as "one of the most original socialist philosophers of the twentieth century,"[26] Henri De Man was mentioned in the same breath as Heidegger as major thinkers of the new fascist order.[27] It is important to remember that practically every European country had its fascist parties. As president of the Belgian Workers' Party, Henri was a promoter of national socialism before the Germans occupied his country. It is easy to understand how his nephew would be pulled into his orbit.

Paul De Man's articles for the fascist periodical *Le Soir* were mainly literary discussions, sometimes with an anti-Semitic theme. "Their cerebralness, their capacity to assimilate doctrines while maintaining a cold detachment from them," he writes, is one of "the specific characteristics of the Jewish mind."[28] De Man distinguishes between his own criticism of the Jews and "vulgar anti-Semitism"—a distinction which his defenders make much of.[29] But his intellectual anti-Semitism is the common theme of fascist theorists, that Jews are to blame not so much for their race as for their ideas. In saying the "Jewish mind" is "cold" and "cerebral," he is echoing the fascist line that blames the Jews for abstractionism, for the alienating effect of monotheism, rationalism, and transcendent morality.

De Man goes on in the same essay to say that "a solution to the

Jewish problem that would lead to the creation of a Jewish colony isolated from Europe would not have, for the literary life of the West, regrettable consequences."[30] Shipping the Jews off to form their own colony was in fact an early Nazi proposal to deal with the "Jewish problem." There was at one point a plan to send them all to Madagascar. The goal of isolating the Jews in one place developed instead into the invention of the concentration camp. After that, the euthanasia facilities would ensure the final "solution to the Jewish problem."

De Man was in the mainstream of fascist intellectualism. These early essays explore themes that he would later develop in his mature writings. The rejection of transcendence, evident in his anti-Jewish remarks, was fundamental to both fascist thought and to deconstruction. A key theme of the early essays, which would be developed in the later works, is anti-individualism.[31] De Man's effort to depersonalize, or even dehumanize, literature is evident as early as 1942, when he wrote in *Le Soir* that

> the development [of literary style] does not depend on arbitrary, personal decisions but is connected to forces which perform their relentless operations across the doings of individuals.[32]

This is a succinct statement, in a fascist intellectual context, of what would later become the postmodernist critique of the self.

De Man's later works acquire a different resonance in light of his early fascism. Stanley Corngold cites the arbitrary violence that characterizes De Man's later works. For example, he quotes a passage from *Allegories of Reading*:

> Writing always includes the moment of dispossession in favor of the arbitrary power play of the signifier; and from the point of view of the subject, this can only be experienced as a dismemberment, a beheading, or a castration.[33]

The act of writing, the simple assertion of meaning, becomes not only a "power play," but an act of "arbitrary power." The use of language is conceived of as an act of violence, the sort of brutal violation routinely practiced by SS medical personnel.

Elsewhere in *Allegories of Reading*, in a discussion of Rousseau's *Confessions*, De Man writes that

> It is always possible to face up to every experience (to excuse any

139

> guilt) because the experience always exists simultaneously as fictional discourse and as empirical event and it is never possible to decide which one of the two possibilities is the right one. The indecision makes it possible to excuse the bleakest of crimes because, as a fiction, it escapes from the constraints of guilt and innocence.[34]

Experience itself is not only an event but a "text," a meaning that has been constructed like any other fiction. Because of the gap between reality and meaning, "the bleakest crimes" can be rationalized. In De Man's case, the gap between the "fictional discourse" that he gave about his life and the "empirical event" of his wartime activities is particularly great.

Deconstruction encourages this kind of moral detachment. It also tends to minimize the past. In a discussion of Nietzsche, De Man wrote that "the bases for historical knowledge are not empirical facts but written texts, even if these texts masquerade in the guise of wars or revolutions."[35] Just as literary texts have no determinate meaning in themselves and are ultimately unknowable, the same must be true of *texts* such as wars and revolutions.

Hirsch sees in De Man's attempt to deconstruct history his personal attempt to evade his own past.[36] But Hirsch argues that it is not just De Man who is trying to hide his complicity with fascism. The intellectual establishment itself is trying to keep hidden "the dark secret that European high culture in its most advanced phase not only was powerless to prevent the construction and implementation of the death camps, but actually provided the ideological base on which the death camps were built."[37]

Some of De Man's followers have been defending him by trying to deconstruct the whole controversy. De Man's journalism is scrutinized for its internal contradictions, so that his attacks on Jews are deconstructed into defenses of Jews. Those who criticize De Man for being a Nazi and an anti-Semite are fed into the deconstructive mill, whereupon De Man's critics are accused of being Nazis and anti-Semites. Such deconstructive apologies for De Man read like macabre self-parodies, their obfuscations and evasions showing how deconstruction is utterly incapable of dealing with genuine historical and moral issues, or of questioning itself.[38]

Two arguments that deconstruction is nonfascist do deserve consideration. It has been pointed out that the major theorist of deconstruction is not De Man but Jacques Derrida, a Jew. Decon-struction thus cannot be essentially fascist. Hirsch dismisses this point as being racist, a recapitulation of the Nazi argument that someone must think in a certain way because of his race. Derrida, he says, has chosen to be a French intellectual, not a Jewish intel-lectual, to follow Heidegger instead of Judaism.[39]

But other scholars, apart from the De Man controversy, have placed Derrida in the Jewish tradition. Susan Handelman, in her book *The Slayers of Moses: The Emergence of Rabbinic Interpretation in Modern Literary Theory*,[40] sees Derrida's approach to interpre-tation as being in some ways analogous to that of the Jewish midrash tradition, with its close attention to the unsystematized nuances of language. This Jewish approach is far different from Hellenic thought, which has dominated Western philosophy with its attempt to go beyond language to posit rational systems and idealized truths. Herbert Schneidau relates Derrida's deconstruction to the radical iconoclasm of the Biblical tradition.[41] G. Douglas Atkins, supporting both Handelman and Schneidau, employs Thorlief Boman's *Hebrew Thought Compared to Greek* to place Derrida in the Hebraic tradition.[42]

If Derrida's thought has a religious dimension, as these critics imply, it is a religion of a particular kind. Derrida's connection to Judaism, as Handelman recognizes, is not any sort of orthodox Ju-daism, but more of a deconstruction of the rabbinic tradition. Al-though deconstruction may have parallels with Biblical iconoclasm, there is a crucial difference. The Hebrew prophets cast down all human-made idols; but they did so on the authority of the Word. God was their "transcendental signified," who communicated His moral absolutes through human language. A deconstructionist may destroy idols, but he goes on to destroy everything else, including the sacred Word. The biblical prototype of the deconstructionist may be King Jehoiakim: He asked for the written words of the prophet. As each passage of the sacred text was read, he would "cut it with the penknife, and cast it into the fire that was on the hearth, until all the roll was consumed in the fire that was on the hearth. Yet [the king and his court] were not afraid, nor rent their garments" (Jeremiah 36:23–24 KJV). The prophetic author marvels not only at Jehoiakim's blasphemy in mutilating and incinerating the Word; he marvels at the complacency of the king and his followers in doing

141

so, as if the Word could be annihilated with no further consequences.

Any religious significance of deconstruction, as Atkins notes, is that of 20th–century radical theology—to Altizer's "Christian atheism" with its rejection of transcendence, and to existential theologians such as Tillich for whom faith must be void of transcendent content.[43] Deconstruction would have to challenge any confessional religion, Jewish or Christian. It would be difficult for a confessional Christian, who must believe in the *Logos*—God's design for creation, His Son, and His Word (John 1:1–14)—to avoid being "logocentric."

A more telling argument against the connection between deconstruction and fascism is that deconstruction calls all authority into question. It thereby undercuts all forms of "totalizing," including totalitarianism. Therefore, deconstruction is intrinsically anti-fascist.[44] The major problem with this argument is that it betrays a lack of understanding about what fascism actually was. Fascism, in its revolutionary phase, was emphatically iconoclastic. The impulse to demolish the ideas and values of Western civilization characterized fascism from Nietzsche through the Futurists through the Storm Troopers. As Nietzsche said, "whoever must be a creator in good and evil, verily, he must first be an annihilator and break values."[45]

Once the fascist power structures were in place, the revolutionary phase was silenced. Deconstructionists would no doubt, at this point, be suppressed. But deconstructive skepticism would have played its role. The deconstruction of language would have undermined reason and would reduce all discourse to propaganda. The deconstruction of the self would have turned liberty into an illusion and would undo the very possibility of human rights. It would have prepared the ground for the "the practical and violent resistance to transcendence" that is fascism.[46]

For deconstructionists, authority is only a mask for power. Fascists would have no problem with that. It is one thing to undermine human authority, but it is another to undermine the higher authority of a transcendent moral law, which could call power into question. With deconstruction, arbitrary power is all that is left.

The moral vacuity of deconstruction is its greatest weakness. Ward Parks, exasperated at the tortuous rationalizations and tiresome inversions of the attempts to deconstruct Paul De Man's fascism, raises the crucial question:

142

> What *is* the deconstructive basis for condemning Nazism? Would it not be in keeping with the logic of deconstruction to reverse a claim like "the Nazis oppressed the Jews," showing instead that the Jew cooked in a Nazi oven was really the Nazis' oppressor?[47]

Deconstruction assaults humanism, but it can put nothing in its place. Deconstruction underestimates "the dangers in unleashing an essentially nihilistic philosophy on human communities that cannot long survive without ethical constraints."[48]

The severest critic of deconstruction may be David Hirsch, whose wife is a Holocaust survivor. He raises questions that probe even deeper, cutting to the fundamental spiritual issues of modern and postmodern thought:

> Is it possible . . . that there should be no connection between the Nazis' effort to murder God in Auschwitz and Heidegger's attempt to deconstruct the metaphysical tradition in Western philosophy, which is to say his attempt to destroy that fusion of Hellenism and Hebraism which is Christianity? In fact, are we not bound in all honesty to say that the real-world endpoint of Heideggerian (and now Derridean and de Manian) deconstruction of the logocentric tradition is precisely Auschwitz?[49]

Goethe's *Faust* begins in the impasse of postmodern skepticism. Faust has mastered all of the intellectual disciplines of the university, "and this is all that I have found—the impossibility of knowledge!"[50] In his struggle to resolve his discrepancy between his idealism and his cynicism, Faust turns to the "master text"—the Bible. Then follows a remarkable passage, which has been said to recapitulate the whole history of Western philosophy and to usher in the modern (and I would say the postmodern) age:[51]

> It is written: In the beginning was the Word.
> Here I am stuck at once. Who will help me on?
> I am unable to grant the Word such merit,
> I must translate it differently
> If I am truly illumined by the spirit.
> It is written: In the beginning was the Mind.
> But why should my pen scour
> So quickly ahead? Consider that first line well.
> Is it the Mind that effects and creates all things?
> It *should* read: In the beginning was the Power

Yet, even as I am changing what I have writ,
Something warns me not to abide by it.
The spirit prompts me, I see a flash what I need,
And write: In the beginning was the Deed![52]

Faust begins by rejecting the authority of the Word of God, going on—like a liberal theologian—to reinterpret the text according to his liking. But in rejecting the authority of the Bible he is also rejecting the authority of language.

Faust first repudiates the primacy of God's language in favor of the primacy of the Mind. Here is the optimism of the Enlightenment, the confidence in the rational design of nature and in the authority of human reason. But if the Mind is not merely a passive recorder but an active creator of meaning, there must be a more fundamental principle: "In the beginning was the Power." Goethe thus anticipates both Nietzsche and Foucault. Faust comes to realize the next inevitable step, that power can only be manifested in concrete action: "In the beginning was the Deed!" This conclusion turns out to be the invocation of the demons. The innocuous little poodle, so small and white and harmless, transforms into Mephistopheles. Faust's "deed" is to commit his soul to the Devil.

Faust's deconstruction of John 1:1, the shifts from language to mind to power to deed, is startlingly prophetic, anticipating Germany's own Faustian experience[53] and the postmodern revival of these very themes. Postmodern thought likewise assumes the "impossibility of knowledge." The Word of God is drained of its transcendent authority. Language itself becomes problematic, turned into a "speech-act," a deed rather than a vehicle for ultimate truth. The Mind loses its authority, as rationality is itself called into question. Contemporary thought is presently at the stage of assuming that Power is the source of all meaning. We await the next stage— *acting* on these assumptions, asserting Power with no moral or even rational restrictions. The utter loss of transcendence will mean not liberation but bondage to demons. While Mephistopheles, with his cynicism and very contemporary sophistication, has his charms, he has a hidden agenda. Postmodernists may find, like Faust and like Faustian Germany, that they are opening themselves up to more than they bargained for.

144

"The People's Culture" Fascism and the Mass Mind

The old goal of modern humanism, the education of the free person, is not sufficiently modern. Beyond the singular "I" exists the "we"; beyond the needs of individuals exists the needs of the community of the people.

—Elfride Heidegger-Petri[1]

We have begun again to structure the primordial feeling, the tribal emotions from which a few centuries of literacy divorced us.

—Marshall McLuhan[2]

Fascism is, of course, more than an intellectual theory. Ideas must spill over into a mass movement and then become translated into political policies and concrete actions. Today, while postmodern thinkers are busy dismantling the Judeo-Christian intellectual heritage, the popular culture is opening itself up to a newly-packaged fascism with an even greater recklessness.

The Image and the Masses

The new electronic media, particularly television, has had a profound impact upon contemporary culture. The centrality of language is giving way to the centrality of the electronic image. As Neil Postman has shown in his studies of the impact of television, responding to words is completely different from responding to visual images. Language appeals to the intellect; images appeal to the emotions. Reading a book requires sustained concentration and logical reflection; a television program, on the other hand, creates an instant emotional response.[3]

This difference between symbols that demand conceptualization and reflection and symbols that evoke feeling has many implications, one of the most important being that the content of the TV curriculum is irrefutable. You can dislike it, but you cannot disagree with it. . . . There is no way to show that the feelings evoked by the imagery of a McDonald's commercial are false, or indeed, true. Such words as *true* and *false* come out of a different universe of symbolism altogether. Propositions are true or false. Pictures are not.[4]

The new media teach its viewers "to search for time-compressed experience, short-term relationships, present-oriented accomplishment, simple and immediate solutions. Thus, the teaching of the media curriculum must lead inevitably to a disbelief in long-term planning, in deferred gratification, in the relevance of tradition, and in the need for confronting complexity."[5] In his book *Amusing Ourselves to Death*, Postman shows how the television mind-set reduces everything—politics, education, religion—to entertainment.[6] Postman warns that this new image-centeredness can have catastrophic effects on a democratic society.

Hitler too was something of a media scholar. After discussing the superiority of public speaking over writing as a means of persuading people, Hitler observes that

the picture in all its forms up to the film has greater possibilities. Here a man needs to use his brains even less; it suffices to look, or at most to read extremely brief texts, and thus many will more readily accept a *pictorial presentation* than *read* an *article* of any *length*. The picture brings them in a much briefer time, I might almost say at one stroke, the enlightenment which they obtain from written matter only after arduous reading.[7]

Here, long before the television age, Hitler anticipates the immediacy of the image, its ability to evade the reason, and its manipulative potential.

The priority of the image over language was a tenet of fascist theory. The *Word*, with its Jewish and Christian connotations, is abstract and transcendent. The *Image*, locus of pagan spirituality, is concrete and immediate. The fascist exaltation of the image over the word is evident from Ezra Pound's literary *imagism* to Heidegger's project of seeking "to conquer the undestroyed naming power of language and word."[8]

The fascist critique of language is another connection to post-modern critical theory. Paul De Man stressed the error of "taking a linguistic construct for a natural reality." "This questioning of the authority of language," said one of his students, "yielded the most subversive pedagogy I know."[9] Rejecting the authority of words is connected to rejecting the authority of the Word.

Nazi rallies often included the burning of books. These were generally carried out not by uneducated mobs but by university students. Bookburnings took place at the University of Freiburg while Heidegger was rector.[10] The demonstrations were parallel to the recent protests at Stanford University. Students, primed with postmodern critical theory, demonstrated against the canon of classic texts required in the basic humanities course. Since the reading list was dominated by "dead white males" and was "Eurocentric," the students protested, chanting "Hey, Hey, Ho, Ho! Western Civ has got to go!" The reading list was changed. The motivation of the students who participated in the bookburning rallies was similar and equally sincere. They sought to strike back at the ideas of Western civilization by destroying the words that expressed them. Deconstruction is even more subversive, stripping the text away of all its authority, interrogating it for its secret crimes, and liquidating its very meaning. Deconstructing a book is very close to burning it.

The Nazis may have burned books, but they loved the visual media. Josef Goebbels, Minister for Public Enlightenment and Propaganda, announced, "I want to exploit the film as an instrument of propaganda." The Third Reich produced 1,363 films. Many were produced for sheer entertainment, with a propaganda subtext—anti-semitic melodramas, historical epics from the folkish culture, action films lauding the military. Many proved critical in shaping public opinion, such as the pro-euthanasia movie *I Accuse.* Some were cinematic masterpieces such as Leni Riefenstahl's *Triumph of the Will* and *Olympia,* a celebration of the Aryan athlete at the Berlin Olympics. No film could be released without official approval. Goebbels, a true movie buff, no matter how busy he was, screened at least one film a day. He also made masterful use of the electronic communication medium of his day, the radio, keeping the country united and enthusiastic in their cause through the darkest days of the war.[11] One wonders what he could have done with television.

Both fascism and today's popular culture are *image-centered.*

Because of the burgeoning media technology, it would be safe to say that contemporary popular culture is far more *image-centered* than Germany of the 1930s and is becoming increasingly so. This suggests that today's population would be even more susceptible to the psychology of propaganda, with its emotional impact and irrational appeals.

Postman has shown how political discourse in the United States has changed from the days of the Lincoln-Douglas debates, which consisted of hours upon hours of close analysis of complex issues, to the *sound bites* and image manipulation of today's media campaigns. Candidates, managed by *image consultants,* are chosen not for much for their competence as for their *media presence* and their *charisma.*[12] Fortunately, most of the persuasive potential of the media is devoted to selling merchandise rather than political ideologies. Still, the enormous influence of television commercials—which largely finance the networks and fuel the whole economy—is evidence of the media's rhetorical power.

The purpose of the mass media for the fascists, however, went beyond propaganda. The goal of fascism was the creation of an organic, mass community. The power of images is that they unite diverse people into one. The individuals in a movie theater join in a common experience, feeling and responding as one. Such a communal experience would help to heal the alienation of the individual. Propaganda was not understood merely as cynical manipulation of the public through lies; it had an important ideological function. Propaganda forged the people into a common will; it created the community.

This was the reason for the mass rallies and the grandiose public rituals. Hitler's party rallies were stunning spectacles. An account of the Nuremberg rally of 1936 describes 140,000 people gathered in grandstands. The moment Hitler arrives, 150 floodlights come on, aimed straight up into the sky, forming "a Gothic cathedral made of light." Then 25,000 flag bearers, uniformed and carrying red banners, solemnly march in out of the darkness, "an undulating stream, red and broad, its surface sparkling with gold and silver, which slowly comes closer like fiery lava." Then a mass choir begins to sing.[13]

Hitler understood well the psychology of the alienated individual who longs to be part of a vast crowd. In a passage in *Mein Kampf*

148

that is remarkable for its combination of poignancy and cynicism, Hitler writes,

> The mass meeting is also necessary for the reason that in it the individual, who at first, while becoming a supporter of a young movement, feels lonely and easily succumbs to the fear of being alone, for the first time gets the picture of a larger community, which in most people has a strengthening, encouraging effect.... In the crowd he always feels somewhat sheltered.... When from his little workshop or big factory, in which he feels very small, he steps for the first time into a mass meeting and has thousands and thousands of people of the same opinions around him, when, as a seeker, he is swept away by three or four thousand others into the mighty effect of suggestive intoxication and enthusiasm, when the visible success and agreement of thousands confirm to him the rightness of the new doctrine and for the first time arouse doubt in the truth of his previous conviction—then he himself has succumbed to the magic influence of what we designate as "mass suggestion."[14]

The bourgeoisie, says Hitler, lack "the psychological instinct for *mass effect* and *mass influence*."[15]

One effect of the today's mass media, it has been suggested, is the creation of a mass culture.[16] The entire nation, and much of the world, watch the same television shows, follow the same fashions, and think in the same ways. Individual differences become homogenized. The world becomes "retribalized." McLuhan's metaphor of the world as a *global village* means more than "it's a small world." McLuhan argues that the electronic media, for all its technical sophistication, is transforming the world back into more primitive, tribal modes of thinking. When images displace language, rationalism and the alienation that it breeds will fade into an information system that will stress experience, emotion, and group identity. The post-literate world will be similar to the preliterate world—spontaneous, affective, communal.[17] McLuhan, having—like modernists from Stravinsky on—a bias towards the primitive, thinks this will be wonderful. In light of the recent large-scale experiment in primitive consciousness that was fascism, we might not think so.

The emergence of a mass culture in Germany meant that *high culture*—the realm of the more sophisicated arts and letters—would have to give way to *popular culture*—the more accessible art forms enjoyed by the masses. German romanticism since Herder had maintained that the high culture of the intellectuals is artificial, whereas the folk culture of the people is genuine.[18] Under the Nazis, this cultural populism acquired even more importance. "German culture has always been a people's culture," wrote one Nazi theorist. "For even if the damage caused by liberal civilization and Jewish alienation has been great, no one has ever succeeded in taking the earth from German culture."[19] Here are the familiar fascist distinctions between *culture* and *civilization,* organic communalism and *Jewish alienation.* The "people's culture" will recover the old folkways and be accessible to all.

Although many artists and intellectuals of the high culture were important supporters of the new *Reich*, especially at first, the formation of a mass consciousness and the achievement of an organic community required a new emphasis on popular art. That is to say, on kitsch. Sentimental poetry, pictures of Rhine Maidens, and lachrymose music became fashionable again.[20] What would seem unutterably tasteless according to the standards of the *high culture* would be measured very differently by the *people's culture*. The complexities of pre-*Reich* expressionism and modernism, while still appreciated by Nazi intellectuals such as Goebbels, had to give way to simpler, more popular art forms suitable to a mass consciousness.

Today, popular culture is again swallowing up the high culture. Kenneth Myers has shown how the media-driven mass culture is pushing out both the high culture and the traditional folk culture. Many children today no longer know the fairy tales or nursery rhymes of their folk culture, but they do know the Scooby-Doo cartoons and the latest advertising jingle. Adults still listen to the rock-and-roll of their adolescence instead of more sophisticated music. Serious art and letters require close attention, knowledge, and active involvement, even work, on the part of its audience. High quality art can hardly compete with the instant accessibility, emotional gratification, and market-driven appeal to the least common denominator demanded by a *people's culture*.

Today's high culture, however, bears much of the blame for the triumph of mediocrity. Today's artistic and academic establishments are purposefully blurring the distinctions between *high culture* and *popular culture*.

150

Postmodern critics are leading the way. Artistic standards and measures of merit are deconstructed as manifestations of social power. According to this line of thought, the ruling "white male Europeans" of high education, income, and social status, determine what is considered *good* and *bad*. This holds true in aesthetic, as well as moral, judgments. Thus, "classic" works of literature such as Shakespeare and Milton are *privileged* over works popular with the disempowered. The approved literary *canon,* consisting mostly of works by dead white European males, supports the values of the power elite. Categories of "aesthetic quality" are devices to label works by women, minorities, and the lower classes (and the kinds of works that they enjoy) as inferior, thus keeping them in their place.

Much of the effort of postmodernist criticism has been to revise the canon, to interrogate the classic authors to reveal their oppressive ideology and to bring into the canon writers and genres of literature that have been *marginalized.* The difference between high culture and popular culture is denied. Types of writing that have been traditionally considered formulaic and nonliterary are considered to be just as worthy of critical attention as the so-called classics. Universities are offering courses, and even academic specialities, in popular culture. Literature departments may offer courses in Harlequin Romances or television soap operas (genres that appeal to women). Monster movies, pulp thrillers, and rock-'n-roll lyrics are subjected to the same earnest critical scrutiny once reserved for the novels of Jane Austen.

The artists of the high culture are themselves selling out to the mass market. This was the significance of Andy Warhol's Campbell Soup cans and Marilyn Monroe prints. Warhol's avant-garde gesture was to reject completely the "high art" tradition, the self-contained experimentations studied in art history textbooks. Warhol turned instead to the traditions of popular art, purposefully imitating its blandness, mass-production, and celebrity-mongering. Moreover, with dizzying levels of irony, Warhol's send-up of pop culture worked, in terms of both the high culture and the low. Warhol's self-conscious and half-mocking playing out of the celebrity role actually made him a celebrity. His parodies of pop commercialism were huge commercial successes. The avant-garde artist became fabulously wealthy.

The mass market promises such huge financial rewards that it is hard for serious artists to resist its allure. Distinguished novelists now live to make the best-seller list. Authors of the "high culture" are now writing westerns, mysteries, and thrillers (throwing in a little knowing irony, perhaps, but not enough to affect sales). The real mark of success, though, is to land a movie contract. Publishers now look for manuscripts not only that people will read but that have potential to be made into movies. Since many publishers and authors make more money on Hollywood deals than they do with their books, Hollywood, a voracious consumer of stories, is driving the publishing industry—another victory of the image over the word.

One danger of any kind of mass consciousness is its proclivity for violence. Crowd psychologists have studied how individual inhibitions are easily lost when a person becomes a part of a mob. Individuals who are personally gentle and kind-hearted can turn murderous when they give up their personalities to that of the larger group. Mobs tend to be governed less by reason than by emotion, less by moral restrictions and more by irrational impulses. That is why Hitler loved them.

Violence

The Nuremberg rally, with 140,000 human beings molded into one, was not only a way to create a sense of mass community; it was also a way to incite that community to violence. This was another function of the whole Nazi propaganda apparatus—to turn the people against the Jews; to mobilize the entire community for total war.

Today's mass culture is similarly enthralled and titillated by violence. For the most part, this is an aestheticized violence, a vicarious thrill from a movie or rock concert. While it as yet has no specific focus or political outlet, there can be little doubt that the violence celebrated by the media is spilling over into reality, with the increases of bizarre criminality and horrific street violence.

The aesthetics of violence once associated only with the fascist avant-garde have now been completely taken over by the popular entertainment industry. Sorel's *Reflections on Violence* and the Futurists' desire to "exalt movements of aggression," "the destructive gesture," and "the slap and the blow with the fist"[21] used to be

152

shocking and controversial. Such an aesthetic would be especially outrageous to the popular culture of the time, which still hewed to the sentimentality and highmindedness associated with Victorianism. But today, the aesthetics of violence is the province of *popular* culture.

Today's mass market movies revel in decapitations, ice picks in the eye, chain saw mutilations, and heavy-bore ammo blasting people's brains out. An entire sub-genre, the slasher movie, consists of nothing more than one episode after another of teenagers and women getting butchered. Even more sophisticated movies are likely to contain an obligatory car being blown up or a bullet in the face.

While popular entertainment has always prized adventure and suspense, requiring certain elements of violence, the new media violence is different from that of the past. Traditional narratives might employ violence as part of a story, providing suspense and catharsis in the context of a larger meaning. In many contemporary films, such as the slasher movies, the violence is all there is. The plots are minimal and seem more so because they are reused from film to film. The sole attraction is to see the special effects technicians outdo each other in simulating new acts of brutality. After awhile, of course, the shock effect wears off, and the murders start to be played for laughs.

More significant is the way the violence is filmed. Traditional horror stories are told from the point of view of the victim. The audience identifies with the "good" characters; the camera shows what the hero is seeing—the face in the window, the monster coming closer and closer. The viewers of the film are momentarily and vicariously scared, but the monster is defeated in the end, and the conclusion is one of emotional and moral closure. The new horror films often assume the point of view of the monster. The camera shows what the killer is seeing—watching a woman through a keyhole, her face as she looks up at the camera and pleads for mercy, the knife seen from the periphery of the camera's vision plunging down into her body. The viewers have a vicarious experience of what it might be like to kill someone. The movie is not scary, because the viewers do not identify with the victims. Instead, depending upon the psyche of the viewer, the movie may be repulsive; it may be thrilling, offering a rush of pleasure from violating a moral taboo;

or it may desensitize the viewer and dehumanize the victims to the point that vicarious murder seems funny.

Hitler's mass rallies, complete with light shows and music, call to mind some of today's grandiose rock concerts. Going to a concert once meant simply hearing an artist perform in person; with the Woodstock phenomenon the concert became an opportunity to participate in a communal experience. Today, many rock concerts have mutated into mass fantasies of violence. Death Metal bands will sing about rape, torture, and mass murder. ("Scream, as I'm killing you.") The pulsating music is accompanied by grisly stage business—beheadings, torture, the killing of animals. At Slayer concerts, they simulate cutting open a woman and tearing out a baby, then throwing it into the crowd. As this is going on, the teenagers (mostly boys) join with the band in violent chanting. Then they start "moshing," or "slam-dancing," a mass dance in which everyone slams into each other as hard as they can.

The first bands to employ the aesthetics of violence, with angry, violent lyrics and the audience slam dancing into each other, were the punk rockers of the 1980s. The cutting edge punk bands pushed the envelope of moral rebellion. Some punk and heavy metal groups found that racist lyrics violated taboos and struck a chord with their audiences. Some punk rockers read *Mein Kampf* and started wearing swastika jewelry, cultivating a Nazi chic.

The Skinhead movement grew, at least partially, out of punk rock. Especially in Europe, working class young people, resenting foreign immigrants and bad economic prospects, shaved their heads and formed neo-Nazi cells. Some have become part of organized fascist parties, such as England's National Front. Similar organizations have sprung up in nearly every European nation. The first fascist parties, as Bertrand de Jouvenel said at the time, were likewise formed by "young men . . . fired by a love of heroism and violence," especially the latter.[22] Like their SA forebears, the Skinheads enjoy hooliganism, from beating up black people to fomenting riots at soccer games. At their rallies, they play punk metal and mosh.[23]

Foucault has praised the violent irrational for its power to overcome "the violence of reason."[24] While Foucault believes that the mad are oppressed by the sane and criminals are oppressed by the law, history has shown that the removal of all restraints of reason and morality leads not to liberation but to fascism.

154

The New Age

This is not to say that American society is necessarily waiting for another Hitler. There are important obstacles to a true fascism taking root in the United States. The Nazi opinion of America in the 1940s shows definite points of incompatibility, some of which have weakened since the observations were made. The Nazi scholar Franz Otto Wrede predicted why German National Socialism will defeat the United States in the war:

> With the debacle that North America is going to experience through this lost war, it inevitably will return to what it always has been: a colonial land. In this war, organic connection will conquer decay and atomization, the inflation of all value. It is the victory of healthy peoples and people families over race chaos ... over the children of liberalism, over capitalist democracy (plutocracy), the victory of personality in organic unity ... with the community against the mass, of culture against pleasure-technique and dullness. Simultaneously [it is] the victory of obligation toward the soil ... over exhausting the soil, devastation from nomadizing farmers, the victory of Nordic fate attitude which perishes upright and unbendingly bears its fate as opposed to the "happy end" of the American trash film.
>
> Germany in this war defends the old culture of Europe not by safeguarding the gates of the museums but by rejuvenating this culture. She defends it in the East against the threat of Americanism, against the world domination of the inferior average. In other words, in effect, she fight against the annihilation of all cultural values by destructive Jewry.[25]

America is not an organic community, but a mixture of races, organized by the rationalistic charters of democracy. Wrede interestingly indicts the United States for its environmental indifference as another sign of its estrangement from nature. The Nazis, as has been mentioned, in their devotion to the "soil," were among the century's first environmental activists. Wrede is also scornful of the sentimentality of the American movies of the time, with their inevitable happy endings. The United States is obsessed with "pleasure-technique" and promotes "the inferior average." All of this, of course—the democracy and the money-making, soil erosion and sappy movies—is the work of the Jew.

American democratic institutions are a genuine barrier to fascism. The American tradition of individualism, which Wrede would consider "atomization," undermines collective communities. The tradition of equality has enabled people of all races and ethnic groups to participate in American society. The American "melting pot," to Wrede, is "race chaos." The legal system, enshrined in the written text of the Constitution, offers a rigorously systematic and decidedly nonorganic process to protect individual rights and to make democracy work—not through a single communal will but through competitive checks and balances. Behind these rights and protections looms the transcendent moral law.

The American system, contrary to what Wrede expected, is still intact. The trivialization of contemporary politics, however, is something to worry about. Hannah Arendt has shown how the fascist approach to politics is a combination of propaganda and terrorism.[26] Democratic politics is becoming more and more susceptible to propaganda as individuals lose interest in governing themselves and as the image replaces the word. Once reason is minimized and there is no longer a moral consensus, there will be no point in rational discussion and moral analysis. Power, as postmodern theorists are saying, becomes everything. The only recourse for someone who is disaffected is the violent exercise of power; that is, to terrorism.

Although there is still some moral consensus in America, this seems to be changing. Utilitarian ethics (what is most useful) and existential ethics (what I choose) have nearly erased the transcendent principles of the Judeo-Christian tradition. Euthanasia has again become morally acceptable to most Americans. The killing of the sick, still forbidden by the legal system which grew from transcendent ethics, is defended on utilitarian grounds (it is too expensive to keep terminally ill people alive) and on existential grounds (I choose to die). Abortion, considered an abhorrent crime a few decades ago, has now become both morally and legally acceptable. Again, the arguments are utilitarian (there are too many mouths to feed) and, with special force, existential (abortion has to remain the mother's choice). It is true that large numbers of Americans continue to hold transcendental ethics and approach these issues very differently (there is an absolute right to life). Nevertheless, in public policy debates and in popular culture, the Judeo-Christian approach to ethical issues seems anachronistic and is not taken seriously. Once ethics become immanent and provisional, rather than transcendent and absolute, it will be more difficult to object to fascist policies.

Religious freedom, in a paradox surprising to some, has enabled the United States to remain a religious nation. The majority of Americans belong to a church or synagogue, and the evidence is strong that faith plays a major role in their lives. This may be the strongest obstacle to fascism—belief in the fact of transcendence, the continuing authority of the Judeo-Christian scriptures.

Religion, however, seems to be changing. The mainline Christian denominations have been turning away from transcendence, Scripture, and confessionalism, for a century. Joining the mainstream of European prefascist theology, these churches have constructed a spirituality based on immanence, cultural activism, and existentialism. Confessional churches committed to a high view of Scripture are flourishing. Yet many of them are shifting their focus on transcendent truths in favor of experience, emotionalism, and communalism. Many Americans are turning to neopagan spiritualities. *New Age* religions combine deification of the self, nature mysticism, and a secularized occultism. Religion may be the surest defense against fascism, but it may also be its point of entry.

America, despite undeniable problems, still is committed, in theory, to the equality of all. Feminism is growing in influence, while Nazism was explicitly masculinist. There were, however, Nazi feminists such as Martin Heidegger's wife, Elfride Heidegger-Petri, who wrote,

> The honorific name of "comrade of the people" that the Führer, in his speech, gave to German women is opposed to any inclination to discriminate against women. . . . Being a woman is not to be a slave. . . . To be woman and mother means to attain spiritual values.[27]

Nevertheless, official Nazi doctrine was opposed to the "emancipation of women," and the values of the *Männerbund* were firmly in place. Whether there could be a feminist version of fascism remains to be seen. Certainly, contemporary feminists have been keen practitioners of deconstruction and other postmodern modes of thought, including attempts to jettison the Judeo-Christian tradition in favor of ancient spiritualities centered in the goddess and in immanent values. The synthesis of fascism and feminism would be a formidable combination.

Racial equality is an important part of America's egalitarian ideal. While great progress was made in the legal system to eliminate racism, enormous problems remain. Racial friction is increasing. Racism festers. Old-line fascists have reemerged to foment racial hate—the American Nazi party; the Ku Klux Klan. There are also new groups that are explicitly fascist in their ideology, emphasizing white supremacy and a revived anti-Semitism: White Aryan Resistance (WAR); Aryan Nation; East Side White Pride; Confederate Hammer Skins; National White Resistance; Bay Area Skinheads; Romantic Violence.[28] These groups remain small and are definitely out of the mainstream, although the growing number of young people in these groups is cause for concern.

Neofascism is an even bigger problem in Europe. The collapse of communism in Eastern Europe and Russia has given way to intense ethnic nationalism. Because of their hatred for communist totalitarianism, most of these ethnic movements oppose any kind of strong centralized government, an important inoculation against genuine fascism.[29] Still, in the economic chaos following the disintegration of communism and fueled by old ethnic hatreds, fascist parties are emerging. These are generally supported by hardline former communists, showing once more the affinity between Marxist and national socialism. Eastern European nations such as Romania and Croatia had native fascist parties of their own in the 1930s. They are coming back to life. An emerging fascist movement in Russia threatens to restore totalitarianism. Neofascist parties are reemerging in Western Europe: the National Front in England; the Vlaams Blok in Belgium; the Freedom Party in Austria; Le Pen's National Front in France; the ubiquitous Skinheads with their swastika graffiti, racial violence, and soccer riots, in London, Berlin, Budapest, and nearly every European city.[30]

Unless economic conditions degenerate to those of Weimar Germany and unless there is a dramatic cultural collapse, such groups are unlikely to seize total power as Hitler did. More likely may be a completely different form of fascism, a fascism with a human face. Communities of expressive, self-actualized people, bound together by the electronic media, will live healthy lives in harmony with nature. Social and intellectual conformity will yield a common will.

Social engineering will direct the birth and education of children. The economy will be planned. Violence may be directed against other communities, or the appetite for violence may be satisfied vicariously through the media. Nature religions—lauding the environment and offering emotional fulfillment—will replace Judaism and Christianity, whose adherents will either adjust their beliefs to make them harmonize with the new faith or else face sterner measures. All will be one. Misfits and the handicapped will be quietly euthanized.

There is no reason any of this has to happen. But avoiding fascism, whether the old version or the new, will take vigilance. We certainly have not seen the last of fascism.

Paul De Man saw the problem very clearly as a fascist journalist. In his article "The Jews in Contemporary Literature," he points out how cultural trends develop largely unaffected by catastrophic events such as world wars:

> It seems that aesthetic evolutions obey very powerful laws that continue on their course even while humanity is shaken by important events. The world war provoked a profound upheaval in the political and economic world. But artistic life has been affected relatively little, and the forms that we know at present follow in a logical and normal fashion those that came before.[31]

De Man was referring to World War I, his argument being that while the Jews were spoiling the rest of post-war Europe, the arts were largely unaffected. What he says, however, seems strikingly applicable to World War II, to De Man's own career, and to the "powerful laws" by which 20th-century arts and letters can spawn a nightmarish ideology, then continue in the same direction, no matter how many people were killed. Wars may not affect the world of ideas, but the world of ideas does affect culture and can produce wars.

The 20th century persists in its obsession with primitive emotions, irrational subjectivity, moral revolt, anti-transcendence, and the triumph of the will. But civilization is fragile. Deep in the human heart is what St. Paul called "the mystery of iniquity," which is barely held in check by the objective restraints of law, reason, and conscience. To eliminate those restraints is to unleash hell on earth.

The assault on the Judeo-Christian tradition is ultimately neither

159

intellectual nor cultural but spiritual. As the Jewish author George Steiner has said,

> By killing the Jews, Western culture would eradicate those who had "invented" God. . . . The holocaust is a reflex, the more complete for being long-inhibited, of natural sensory consciousness, of instinctual polytheistic and animist needs.[32]

Fascism is the modern world's nostalgia for paganism. It is a sophisticated culture's revolt against God.

Notes

Chapter 1: "A Disease of the Times"
(pp. 16–24)

1. George Steiner, *In Bluebeard's Castle: Some Notes Towards the Redefinition of Culture* (New Haven, CT: Yale Univ. Press, 1971), p. 41.
2. David H. Hirsch, *The Deconstruction of Literature: Criticism after Auschwitz* (Hanover, NH: Brown Univ. Press, 1991), p. 71.
3. "Dieser Friede," *Gesammelte Werke*, 12:930. Quoted from Ernst Nolte, *Three Faces of Fascism: Action Française, Italian Fascism, National Socialism*, trans. Leila Vennewitz (New York: Holt, Rinehart & Winston, 1965), p. 7.
4. Essay on Nietzsche, *Gesammelte Werke*, 9:702. Quoted from Nolte, p. 7.
5. Nolte, p. 429. See his section, "Fascism as a Metapolitical Phenomenon," pp. 429–462. See also the discussion of Nolte's thesis in Zeev Sternhall, "Fascist Ideology," in *Fascism: A Reader's Guide: Analyses, Interpretations, Bibliography*, ed. Walter Laqueur (Berkeley: University of California Press, 1976),pp. 368–369. Hirsch is very critical of Nolte as a Heideggerian and as a revisionist (see pp. 18, 100, 141–142). Hirsch accuses Nolte of trivializing Auschwitz by making it only another example of human cruelty and by urging Germany to forget its Nazi past. Hirsch is attacking Nolte for an article he wrote, "The Past That Will Not Pass Away," *Frankfurter Allgemeine Zeitung*, 6 June 1986. Hirsch does not take issue with Nolte's earlier scholarship as reflected in *Three Faces of Fascism*.
6. For the social conservatism of mythological cultures and the contrast with the Biblical tradition, see Herbert Schneidau, *Sacred Discontent: The Bible and Western Tradition* (Berkeley: Univ. of California Press, 1977).
7. Victor Farias, *Heidegger and Nazism*, tr. Paul Burrell (Philadelphia: Temple University Press, 1989). For responses to the revelations in Farias's book, see Paul Gottfried, "Heidegger and the Nazis," *The Salisbury Review*, September 1988, pp. 34–38 and Thomas Sheehan, "Heidegger and the Nazis," *The New York Review of Books*, 16 June 1988, pp. 38–47.
8. See Paul De Man, *Wartime Journalism: 1939–1943*, ed. Werner Hamacher, et al. (Lincoln: Univ. of Nebraska Press, 1988). For the reactions to these disclosures, see Werner Hamacher, et al., ed. *Responses on Paul De Man's Wartime Journalism* (Lincoln: Univ. of Nebraska Press, 1989).
9. Foreword to Alastair Hamilton, *The Appeal of Fascism: A Study of Intellectuals and Fascism, 1919–1945* (New York: Macmillan, 1971), p. x.
10. See Volodymyr Odajnyk, *Jung and Politics* (New York: New York Univ. Press,

1976), pp.86–108, and Gerhard Wehr, *Jung: A Biography,* tr. David M. Weeks (Boston: Shambhala, 1982), pp. 304–330.

11. See George Grant, *Grand Illusions: The Legacy of Planned Parenthood* (Brentwood, TN: Wolgemuth and Hyatt, 1988), pp. 90–94.

12. Robert Casillo, *The Genealogy of Demons: Anti-Semitism, Fascism, and the Myths of Ezra Pound* (Evanston, IL: Northwestern Univ. Press, 1988), p. 328. See also p. 22.

13. Hirsch, p. 267.

14. Hirsch, p. 161.

Chapter 2: "The Doctrine of Our Age"
(pp. 25–42)

1. From Mussolini's *Fascism: Doctrine and Institutions,* 31.34.n2. Quoted from Zeev Sternhell, "Fascist Ideology" in Walter Laqueur, ed. *Fascism: A Reader's Guide* (Berkeley: Univ. of California Press, 1976), p. 318.

2. Sternhell, p. 315.

3. See Alvin H. Rosenfeld, *Imagining Hitler* (Bloomington: Indiana Univ. Press, 1985), pp. 103–112.

4. David H. Hirsch, *The Deconstruction of Literature: Criticism after Auschwitz* (Hanover, NH: Brown University Press, 1991), p. 69.

5. Sternhell, p. 316.

6. Sternhell, pp. 353–354.

7. Jaroslav Krejci, "Introduction: Concepts of Right and Left," in *Neo-Fascism in Europe,* ed. Luciano Cheles, et al. (London: Longman, 1991), p. 7.

8. Krejci, pp. 1–2.

9. Krejci, pp. 1–2.

10. Insofar as American conservatives stress the need for traditional morality and are suspicious of institutional change, they would be on the "right." Liberals tend to stress personal freedom over traditional morality, which would put them on the "left." The point is not where to place American liberals and conservatives—which are also probably inadequate metaphors. Rather, the point is that sorting out positions by such metaphorical models results in oversimplification and misunderstanding.

11. Krejci, p. 6.

12. The discussion that follows is indebted to Robert P. Ericksen, *Theologians Under Hitler: Gerhard Kittel, Paul Althaus and Emanuel Hirsch* (New Haven, CT: Yale Univ. Press, 1985), who shows how fascism is a reaction to "the crisis of modernity" and how it developed in response to three cultural forces: the industrial revolution; the democratic revolution; and an intellectual revolution.

13. "Milton," l. 8 and "London."

14. "God's Grandeur," ll. 6–8.

15. "The Tables Turned," l. 28.

16. See *The Social Contract*, Book I. Chapters vi, vii; II. i–v, viii–x; III. ii, vi. Rousseau's theory of the organic state anticipates in surprising detail the theory and practice of fascism.

17. "In Memoriam," stanza LVI, l. 15.

18. Sternhell, p. 322.

19. Sternhell, p. 322.

20. Ericksen, p. 3.

21. Sternhell, p. 323. For the change in the sciences and humanities from egalitarianism see also pp. 329–330.

22. Sternhell, p. 322.

23. Sternhell, p. 321.

24. Sternhell, p. 323.

25. Sternhell, p. 323.

26. Sternhell, p. 322.

27. Ericksen, pp. 4–5.

28. Sternhell, p. 321.

29. Sternhell, pp. 326–327.

30. Sternhell, p. 339.

31. See Sternhell, pp. 353–357.

32. Sternhell, pp. 326–327.

33. Quoted in Sternhell, p. 328.

34. Sternhell, p. 335.

35. Sternhell, p. 328.

36. Sternhell, pp. 336–337. For the elder De Man's economic theory, see Reed Way Dasenbrock, "Paul De Man: The Modernist as Fascist," in *Fascism, Aesthetics, and Culture,* ed. Richard J. Golsan (Hanover, NH: University Press of New England, 1992), pp. 235–237.

37. Nolte, pp. 8–9.

38. Sternhell, 346. See his discussion of this point on pp. 344–347.

39. Sternhell, p. 345.

40. Sternhell, p. 344.

41. See Hirsch, p. 17.

42. See Hirsch, pp. 161–163, 255–257, and Sternhell, p. 344.

43. Sternhell, p. 345.

44. Sternhell, pp. 346–347.

45. Robert Casillo, *The Genealogy of Demons: Anti-Semitism, Fascism, and the Myths of Ezra Pound* (Evanston, IL: Northwestern Univ. Press, 1988), pp. 75–76.

46. Sternhell, p. 341.

47. Sternhell, pp. 317, 356–357.

48. Sternhell, p. 324. The "sterility" and "dryness" that the fascists believed characterized Jewish thought would typically be ascribed to the fact that the Jews were people of the desert.

49. Sternhell, p. 341.

50. See R. H. Dominick, "The Nazis and Nature Conservationists," *Historian*, 49 (1987): 509–538.

51. Adolf Hitler, *Mein Kampf*, tr. Ralph Manheim (Boston: Houghton Mifflin, 1943), p. 384.

52. Simopekka Virkkula, "One Man's War," *Books from Finland*, 24 (1990): 45–50. The article is a review of Pentti Linkola's book *Johdatus 1990-luvun a jatteluun* [*Introduction to the Thought of the 1990's*] (Helsinki: WSOY, 1989).

53. Quoted by Virkulla, p. 45.

54. Sternhell, p. 332.

55. Martin Heidegger, "The Self-Assertion of the German University [The Rectoral Address]," in Günther Neske and Emil Kettering, ed., *Martin Heidegger and National Socialism: Questions and Answers*, tr. Lisa Harries and Joachim Neugroschel (New York: Paragon House, 1990), p. 13.

56. Quoted in Farias, p. 224.

57. See "The *Spiegel* Interview," for Heidegger's late views on democracy, environmentalism, and technology, printed in Neske, pp. 54–56.

58. Hirsch, p. 162.

59. Quoted in Sternhell, p. 356.

60. Hitler, p. 534.

61. See Hirsch, pp. 258–259.

Chapter 3: "The Hebrew Disease"
(pp. 43–55)

1. "The Twilight of the Idols" in *The Portable Nietzsche*, tr. Walter Kaufmann (New York: Viking Press, 1968), p. 504–505.

2. George Steiner, *The Portage of San Cristobal of A. H.* (New York: Simon and Schuster, 1981), p. 166. See also his book *In Bluebeard's Castle: Some Notes Towards the Redefinition of Culture* (New Haven, CT: Yale Univ. Press, 1971), pp. 36–47.

3. Hannah Arendt, *The Origins of Totalitarianism* (New York: Harcourt, Brace & World, 1951), pp. 3–120.

4. Ernst Nolte, *Three Faces of Fascism: Action Française, Italian Fascism, National Socialism*, trans. Leila Vennewitz (New York: Holt, Rinehart & Winston, 1965), p. 429.

5. Paul De Man, "The Jews in Contemporary Literature," *Le Soir,* 4 March 1941. Translated by David Lehman and printed in his book *Signs of the Times: Deconstruction and the Fall of Paul De Man* (New York: Poseidon Press, 1991), p. 270. In the essay, De Man distances himself from "vulgar anti-Semitism" in favor of a more intellectual anti-Semitism. De Man's defenders, remarkably, find this praiseworthy, as if hating the Jews for intellectual reasons is somehow nobler than hating them out of blind prejudice. The vulgar anti-Semitism of the popular tradition was indeed brutal, and it was easily manipulated by the intellectual anti-Semites who were the designers of the Final Solution. Scholars

have studied the traditions of popular anti-Semitism, but the intellectual anti-Semitism of the National Socialists is less well known and deserves more attention.

6. Quoted from Robert Casillo, *The Genealogy of Demons: Anti-Semitism, Fascism, and the Myths of Ezra Pound* (Evanston, IL: Northwestern Univ. Press, 1988), pp. 30–31, from *The Spirit of Romance*, p. 95. For a thorough discussion of fascism's anti-monotheism, see Casillo, pp. 25–37.

7. Quoted from Casillo, pp. 30–31, from *Selected Prose of Ezra Pound 1909–1965*, p. 51.

8. See Casillo, p. 30.

9. Nolte, p. 430.

10. Casillo, p. 126.

11. Adolf Hitler, *Mein Kampf*, tr. Ralph Manheim (Boston: Houghton Mifflin, 1943), p. 287.

12. Casillo, p. 31. He cites Pound's *Guide to Kulchur*, p. 164; and *Selected Prose*, pp. 58, 150.

13. Casillo, p. 30.

14. Casillo, p. 29.

15. Hitler, p. 454.

16. For the distinction between mythological cultures and Biblical cultures, and how the Hebrews made social criticism possible, see Herbert Schneidau, *Sacred Discontent: The Bible and Western Tradition* (Berkeley: Univ. of California Press, 1976).

17. Quoted in Nolte, p. 124. This thesis, according to Nolte, was also advanced in France by Bernard Lazare and in Germany by Hermann Cohen. The social disruptiveness of Judaism and Christianity, as compared to a pagan civil religion, was also a theme of Rousseau. See *The Social Contract*, Book IV, chapter viii.

18. Nolte, p. 430.

19. Casillo, p. 129.

20. Casillo, p. 129.

21. Alice Yaeger Kaplan, "Paul de Man, *Le Soir*, and the Francophone Collaboration (1940–1942)," in *Responses*, p. 272.

22. Nolte, pp. 406–407, citing Hitler's *Table Talk*. Hitler's analysis of Christianity as the revolt of the slaves is taken from Nietzsche.

23. *Mein Kampf*, p. 454.

24. Quoted in Casillo, p. 32, from *Literary Essays of Ezra Pound*, pp. 150–154.

25. Quoted in Casillo, p. 128, from *Guide to Kulchur*, p. 38.

26. Quoted in Casillo, p. 52, from *Letter*, p. 52.

27. See Nolte, pp. 420–421.

28. Nolte, pp. 406–407, citing Hitler's *Table Talk*.

29. Nolte, p. 138.

30. Casillo, p. 35.

31. Victor Farias, *Heidegger and Nazism*, tr. Paul Burrell (Philadelphia: Temple Univ. Press, 1989), pp. 179–180.

32. Hirsch, p. 266.

33. Farias, pp. 179–180.

34. See Farias, pp. 177–187.

35. Farias, pp. 179–180. For Engelbert Krebs, his views on Heidegger, and his leadership of the Catholic resistance movement, see the letter by Hans Gottschalk in Günther Neske and Emil Kettering, ed., *Martin Heidegger and National Socialism: Questions and Answers* (New York: Paragon House, 1990), p. 172.

36. Casillo, p. 35.

37. Casillo, pp. 32–33.

38. Quoted in Nolte, p. 138.

39. Nolte, pp. 121–122.

40. Quoted in Nolte, p. 124, from *Vers l'Espagne de Franco*, p. 113.

41. Paul Gottfried, "Heidegger and the Nazis," *The Salisbury Review*, September 1988, p. 35.

42. Raymond F. Surburg, "The Influence of the Two Delitzches on Biblical and Near Eastern Studies," *Concordia Theological Quarterly*, 47 (1983): 233–234.

43. Quoted in Surburg, p. 235, from *Die Grosse Taeuschung* (*The Great Deception*), p. 52.

44. Surburg, p. 236.

45. Surburg, p. 236.

46. Surburg, pp. 232–234, 237–238.

47. Robert P. Ericksen, *Theologians under Hitler: Gerhard Kittel, Paul Althaus and Emanuel Hirsch* (New Haven, CT: Yale Univ. Press, 1985), p. 50.

48. See H. Richard Niebuhr, *Christ and Culture* (New York: Harper & Row, 1951), pp. 83–115.

49. Ericksen, p. 203 n81.

50. Casillo, p. 80.

Chapter 4: "Two Masters"
(pp. 56–77)

1. Thomas Altizer, *Gospel of Christian Atheism* (New York: Collins, 1967), p. 136.

2. Adolf Hitler, *Mein Kampf*, tr. Ralph Manheim (Boston: Houghton Mifflin, 1943), p. 114.

3. Shelley Baranowski, *The Confessing Church, Conservative Elites, and the Nazi State* (Lewiston, NY: E. Mellan Press, 1986), p. 58.

4. See Ernst Christian Helmreich, *The German Churches Under Hitler: Background, Struggle, and Epilogue* (Detroit: Wayne State Univ. Press, 1979), pp. 237–301.

5. Max Weinreich, *Hitler's Professors: The Part of Scholarship in Germany's Crimes Against the Jewish People* (New York: Yiddish Scientific Institute, 1946), pp. 62–65.

6. Helmreich, p. 234.

7. Robert P. Ericksen, *Theologians under Hitler: Gerhard Kittel, Paul Althaus, and*

NOTES

Emanuel Hirsch (New Haven, CT: Yale Univ. Press, 1985), p. 48.

8. Quoted in Helmreich, p. 150.

9. Eberhard Bethge, "Troubled Self-Interpretation and Uncertain Reception in the Church Struggle," in *The German Church Struggle and the Holocaust*, ed. Franklin H. Littell and Hubert G. Locke (Detroit: Wayne State Univ. Press, 1974), p. 171.

10. Quotations from the Barmen Declaration are taken from *The Encyclopedia of American Religions: Religious Creeds*, ed. J. Gordon Melton (Detroit: Gale Research Company, 1988), pp. 249–251.

11. Arthur C. Cochrane, "The Message of Barmen for Contemporary Church History," in Littell, pp. 194–195.

12. Quoted in Cochrane, p. 194.

13. Ericksen, pp. 25–26.

14. See the appended biography by J. T. E. Renner in Hermann Sasse, *We Confess: Jesus Christ*, tr. Norman Nagel (St. Louis: Concordia Publishing House, 1984), p. 101. For Sasse's resistance to the German Christians, see Franklin H. Littell, "Church Struggle and Holocaust," in Littell, p. 25. Sasse, interestingly, criticized the Barmen Declaration for its "false ecumenism and Barthian church diplomacy based on Reformed theology" (Renner, p. 101). For Sasse, the Confessions of the Lutheran Reformation were sufficient.

15. Franklin H. Littell, "Church Struggle and the Holocaust," in Littell, p. 25.

16. Littell, p. 25.

17. Ericksen, pp. 123, 120.

18. Ericksen, p. 81.

19. Ericksen, p. 139.

20. Ericksen, pp. 132–134.

21. Ericksen, pp. 178–183.

22. Ericksen, pp. 178–185.

23. Quoted in Morris Ashcraft, *Rudolf Bultmann* (Waco, TX: Word Books, 1972), p. 17.

24. See Helmreich's book for a detailed account of the ecclesiastical conflicts.

25. Wilhelm Niemöller, "The Niemöller Archives," in Littell, p. 53.

26. *The Book of Concord*, tr. Theodore Tappert (Philadelphia: Fortress Press, 1959), p. 38.

27. Ericksen, p. 33. The issue of how to consider Jewish converts to Christianity was a key test in the controversy between the *German Christians* and the *Confessing Church*. For the latter, baptism and faith in Christ define a Christian. For the Nazis, Jewishness is a matter of race. Jewish Christians were to be persecuted like all other Jews.

28. Hitler, *Mein Kampf*, p. 113.

29. Helmreich, p. 338.

30. Quoted in Helmreich, p. 331.

31. Quoted in Helmreich, p. 331.

32. Helmreich, p. 215.

33. Helmreich, p. 215.

34. Niemöller, p. 53; Helmreich, p. 358.

35. Helmreich, pp. 345–346.

36. Niemöller, p. 53.

37. See Helmreich, pp. 336–339, for the problems that the *German Christians* had with the regime.

38. Quoted in Weinreich, p. 67.

39. Quoted in Helmreich, p. 303.

40. See Helmreich, pp. 138–139, 532–533 n.

41. Quoted in Helmreich, p. 285.

42. From *Hitler's Tabletalk* (December 1941), quoted in *The Nazi Years: A Documentary History*, ed. Joachim Remak (Prospect Heights, IL: Waveland Press, 1990), p. 105.

43. Helmreich, p. 220.

44. Quoted in Helmreich, p. 219.

45. Quoted in Helmreich, p. 218.

46. See Helmreich, pp. 319–323.

47. Helmreich, pp. 221, 320.

48. Helmreich, pp. 320–321, who shows that such new rituals were not popular and were unable to displace the Christian rites.

49. Helmreich, p. 153.

50. Quoted in Helmreich, p. 267. Horst Wessel was the composer of the party anthem. Baldur von Schirach was the Reich Youth Leader. See Hermann Glaser, *The Cultural Roots of National Socialism* (Austin: Univ. Texas Press, 1978), pp. 43, 56n.

51. Quoted in Helmreich, p. 201.

52. Helmreich, p. 180.

53. Helmreich, p. 292. Such overt neopaganism caused such an uproar among ordinary German farmers that the almanac was repudiated. Few citizens returned to the solstice rites. Clearly, Christianity was too deeply rooted for the time being, but the spiritual direction of the party was clear.

54. Volodymyr Walter Odajnyk, *Jung and Politics* (New York: New York Univ. Press, 1976), pp. 87–89. For Jung's flirtation with and later repudiation of fascism, see Odajnyk, pp. 86–108, and the chapter "National Socialism: 'Yes, I Slipped Up,'" in Gerhard Wehr, *Jung: A Biography*, tr. David M. Weeks (Boston: Shambhala, 1982), pp. 304–330.

55. J. Stroup, "Political Theology and Secularization Theory in Germany, 1918–1939: Emanuel Hirsch as a Phenomenon of His Time," *Harvard Theological Review*, 80 (1987): 323.

56. Nolte, p. 429.

57. Quoted in Littell, p. 22.

58. Littell, p. 23.

59. Littell, p. 24.

60. For a discussion of philosophic irrationalism and its connections to both fascism and modern theology, see Ericksen, pp. 1–27.

61. Altizer, p. 136.

62. Martin Heidegger, "The Rectorate 1933/34," in Günther Neske and Emil Kettering, ed., *Martin Heidegger and National Socialism: Questions and Answers,* tr. Lisa Harries and Joachim Neugroschel (New York: Paragon House, 1990), p.18.

63. Nolte, p. 429.

64. Elie Wiesel, "Talking and Writing and Keeping Silent," in Littell, p. 271. Richard L. Rubenstein's essay, "Some Perspectives on Religious Faith after Auschwitz," is also printed in Littell, pp. 256–268.

65. Wiesel, p. 273.

66. Quoted in Helmreich, p. 345.

Chapter 5: "The Triumph of the Will"
(pp. 78–93)

1. Martin Heidegger, "The Self-Assertion of the German University [The Rectoral Address]," in Günther Neske and Emil Kettering, ed., *Martin Heidegger and National Socialism: Questions and Answers,* tr. Lisa Harries and Joachim Neugroschel (New York: Paragon House, 1990), p. 13.

2. Martin Luther, *The Bondage of the Will,* tr. Henry Cole (Grand Rapids, MI: Baker, 1976), p. 138.

3. Elie Wiesel, "In the Footsteps of Shimon Dubnov," *Modern Language Studies,* 16 (1986): 105. Cited by David H. Hirsch, *The Deconstruction of Literature: Criticism after Auschwitz* (Hanover, NH: Brown Univ. Press, 1991), p. 72.

4. Jaroslav Krejci, "Introduction: Concepts of Right and Left," in *Neo-Fascism in Europe,* ed. Luciano Cheles, et al. (London: Longman, 1991), p. 6.

5. Rudy Koshar, "From *Stammtisch* to Party: Nazi Joiners and the Contradictions of Grass Roots Fascism in Weimar Germany," *Journal of Modern History,* 59 (1987): 9.

6. *Die Zerstörung der Vernunft* [*The Destruction of Reason*] (Berlin, 1954), p. 5. Cited in Ernst Nolte, *Three Faces of Fascism: Action Français, Italian Fascism, National Socialism,* trans. Leila Vennewitz (New York: Holt, Rinehart, & Winston, 1965), p. 7. Jaspers, however, resisted the Nazis.

7. Hirsch, p. 77.

8. Max Weinreich, *Hitler's Professors: The Part of Scholarship in Germany's Crimes against the Jewish People* (New York: Yiddish Scientific Institute, 1946), p. 7.

9. Weinreich, p. 241.

10. Weinreich, p. 7.

11. See Jean-Paul Sartre and his refusal to tell one of his students whether he should join the Resistance, in *Existentialism and Humanism,* tr. Philip Mairet (Brooklyn, NY: Haskell House, 1977), pp. 35–38.

12. Nolte, p. 429.

13. Nolte, p. 445. See also p. 544 n. 56.

14. Alfred Bamer, quoted by Victor Farias, *Heidegger and Nazism,* tr. Paul Burrell (Philadelphia: Temple Univ. Press, 1989), p. 253.

15. See Nolte, p. 442, et passim.
16. The phrase comes from and is developed in Nietzsche's "The Genealogy of Morals." See Nolte, p. 7.
17. "The Twilight of the Gods" in *The Portable Nietzsche*, tr. Walter Kaufmann (New York: Viking Press, 1968), p. 505. In the context of the passage, Nietzsche is contrasting Judeo-Christian religion with the caste system of Indian religion, which is based on distinct hierarchy and biological breeding. India, of course, was the home of the ancient *Aryans*. Although Nietzsche is critical of Aryan religion also, his conclusion must have had special resonance for his Nazi readers: "Christianity, sprung from Jewish roots and comprehensible only as a growth on this soil, represents the counter-movement to any morality of breeding, of race, of privilege: it is the *anti-Aryan* religion par excellence" (pp. 504–505). See also Nolte, p.444.
18. See Nolte, p. 444.
19. The phrase comes from Nietzsche's "The Gay Science," and is developed in "Thus Spoke Zarathustra."
20. "Ecce Homo," in Friedrich Nietzsche, *Basic Writings,* tr. Walter Kaufmann (New York: Modern Library, 1968), p. 765. See Nolte, p. 443.
21. "Die Unschuld des Werdens," quoted in Nolte, p. 445.
22. "The Anti-Christ" in *Portable Nietzsche,* p. 570. See Nolte, p. 445.
23. J. Stroup, "Political Theology and Secularization Theory in Germany, 1918–1939: Emanuel Hirsch as a Phenomenon of His Time," *Harvard Theological Review*, 80 (1987): 324.
24. Heidegger, "The Self-Assertion of the German University," p. 8.
25. Heidegger, "The Self-Assertion of the German University." p. 10.
26. Hans Schemm, quoted in Hermann Glaser, *The Cultural Roots of National Socialism*, tr. Ernest A. Menze (Austin: Univ. of Texas Press, 1978), p. 99.
27. See, for example, the introduction and various essays collected in Neske, ed., *Martin Heidegger and National Socialism: Questions and Answers.* The "answers" are the attempts to vindicate Heidegger. See also Tom Rockmore, *On Heidegger's Nazism and Philosophy* (Berkeley: Univ. of California Press, 1992). Rockmore's book, which appeared when this present volume was already in press, is perhaps the best treatment of the controversy, sifting the evidence and detailing the influence of fascism on Heidegger's philosophy. Rockmore's conclusions, based on far more detailed philosophical analysis, support my own.
28. Farias, p. 175.
29. See Farias, pp. 177–187.
30. "The Night of the Long Knives" was purportedly how Röhm was describing his planned uprising and coup attempt. The term, used by Hitler in describing Röhm's plans, became transferred to the reign of terror designed to wipe out the alleged conspiracy. The term was later applied to other pogroms. See Louis Snyder, *Encyclopedia of the Third Reich* (New York: McGraw-Hill, 1976), pp. 31–33, 297–298.
31. See Snyder, pp. 31–33, 297–298.
32. Farias, p. 67. For other Nazi elements in *Being and Time*, see Farias, pp. 60–64, and Rockmore, passim..

33. Hirsch, p. 262.
34. Hirsch, p. 86.
35. A. Lewkowitz, "Vom Sinn des Seins: Zur Existenzphilosophie Heideggers," *Monatsschrift für Geschichte und Wissenschaft des Judentums* (Breslau), 80 (1936): 187. Quoted in Farias, pp. 111–112.
36. Heidegger, "The Self-Assertion of the German University," p. 9. See Farias, p. 102.
37. See "Beyond Good and Evil" and "Thus Spoke Zarathustra." For a discussion of Nietzsche's concept of the will to power, see Laurence Lampert, *Nietzsche's Teaching: An Interpretation of "Thus Spoke Zarathustra"* (New Haven, CT: Yale Univ. Press, 1986), pp. 245–254.
38. Heidegger, "The Self-Assertion of the German University." p. 9. See Farias, p. 99.
39. See Farias, p. 102.
40. Quoted in Farias, p. 63.
41. Adolf Hitler, *Mein Kampf*, tr. Ralph Manheim (Boston: Houghton Mifflin, 1943), p. 416.
42. Hitler, *Mein Kampf*, p. 610.
43. Hitler, *Mein Kampf*, p. 475.
44. Reported from a personal interview with Riefenstahl by Robert Jay Lifton, *The Nazi Doctors: Medical Killing and the Psychology of Genocide* (New York: Basic Books, 1986), p. 507 n. 14. For Leni Riefenstahl's role in Hitler's Germany, see Snyder, pp. 296–297.
45. So described on the back cover of Luther's *The Bondage of the Will*, tr. Henry Cole (Grand Rapids, MI: Baker, 1976).
46. Hitler's *Tischgespräche* was not published until after the war, but the very project of his followers writing down his dinner-table conversation is taken directly from Luther. In Hitler's *Table Talk,* his diatribes against Christianity and the church are particularly open and venomous. See Henry Picker and Heinrich Hoffmann, ed., *Hitler's Tischgespräche* (Bonn, 1951). An abridgement was translated into English by Nicholas Fry, under the title *Hitler Close-Up* (New York: Macmillan, 1969).
47. I am indebted for this point and for the analysis of Riefenstahl film to my late colleague Prof. William Houser, to whom this book is dedicated.
48. Luther, *Bondage of the Will*, p. 138.
49. Luther, *Bondage of the Will*, p. 337.
50. See Luther's *The Freedom of a Christian Man* for his explorations of the paradoxes of freedom in those who are both redeemed and fallen.

Chapter 6: "Life Unworthy of Life"
(pp. 94–112)

1. Robert Jay Lifton, *The Nazi Doctors: Medical Killing and the Psychology of Genocide* (New York: Basic Books, 1986), p. 21.

2. Quoted in Victor Farias, *Heidegger and Nazism*, tr. Paul Burrell (Philadelphia: Temple Univ. Press, 1989), pp. 205–206.

3. Quoted by George Steiner, *In Bluebeard's Castle: Some Notes Towards the Redefinition of Culture* (New Haven, CT: Yale Univ. Press, 1971), p. 36.

4. See William Kirk Kilpatrick, *Psychological Seduction* (Nashville, TN: Thomas Nelson, 1983), pp. 107–121. See also John S. Stewart, "Problems and Contradictions of Values Clarification," *Moral Education: It Comes with the Territory*, ed. David Purpel and Keven Ryan (Berkeley, CA: McCutchan, 1976), pp. 136–151.

5. Robert P. Ericksen, *Theologians Under Hitler: Gerhard Kittel, Paul Althaus and Emanuel Hirsch* (New Haven, CT: Yale Univ. Press, 1985), p. 24.

6. Jean Paul Sartre, *Existentialism and Humanism*, tr. Philip Mairet (Brooklyn, NY: Haskell House, 1977), p. 38.

7. As a prisoner, Genet had attracted the attention of Sartre and other distinguished authors with his strikingly original, though violent and pornographic, writing. They exerted their influence to have him released from a life sentence. Genet became a respected novelist and achieved particular success as an Absurdist playwright and founder of the "Theatre of Hatred." See Bettina Knapp, *Jean Genet* (Boston: Twayne, 1989).

8. See the chapter "With the Maoists" in Ronald Hayman, *Sartre: A Life* (New York: Simon and Schuster, 1987), pp. 437–453.

9. See Georges Chatterton-Hill, *The Philosophy of Nietzsche: An Exposition and an Appreciation* (New York: Haskell House, 1914), pp. 268–269, who goes on to discuss Nietzsche's idea of willing one's fate, of personally choosing what is inevitably determined.

10. "Thus Spoke Zarathustra," II.12, in *The Portable Nietzsche*, tr. Walter Kaufmann (New York: Viking Press, 1968), p. 226.

11. "Twilight of the Idols," in *The Portable Nietzsche*, pp. 499–501.

12. Quoted in Farias, pp. 205–206.

13. See Zeev Sternhell, "Fascist Ideology," in *Fascism: A Reader's Guide: Analyses, Interpretations, Bibliography* (Berkeley: Univ. of California Press, 1976), p. 317.

14. David H. Hirsch, *The Deconstruction of Literature: Criticism after Auschwitz* (Hanover, NH: Brown Univ. Press, 1991), p. 159.

15. *Freiheit, Gleicheit, Sterblichkeit* (Stuttgart, 1982), pp. 26–41. Quoted in Farias, p. 62.

16. Michael Curtis, *Three Against the Third Republic: Sorel, Barres, and Maurras* (Princeton, NJ: Princeton Univ. Press, 1959), p. 116.

17. Sternhell, p. 332.

18. Sternhell, p. 339.

19. Quoted in Farias, pp. 138–139.

20. From "Canto XXX," in Ezra Pound, *Selected Poems* (New York: New Directions, 1957), p. 125. See also the discussion of this poem in Robert Casillo, *The Genealogy of Demons: Anti-Semitism, Fascism, and the Myths of Ezra Pound* (Evanston, IL: Northwestern Univ. Press, 1988), pp. 144–145.

21. "The Antichrist," in *The Portable Nietzsche*, pp. 572–573. Cf. Hitler in *Mein Kampf*, (Boston: Houghton Mifflin, 1943), pp. 132, 247, 287–289.

22. Pound, from "Canto XXX," p. 126.

23 See George L. Mosse, *Nationalism and Sexuality: Respectability and Abnormal Sexuality in Modern Europe* (New York: Howard Fertig, 1985), pp. 175–176.

24. See Mosse, pp. 153–162. See also Hermann Glaser, *The Cultural Roots of National Socialism*, tr. Ernest A. Menze (Austin: Univ. of Texas, 1978), p. 132.

25. See Hitler, *Mein Kampf*, pp. 251–254. For his tolerance of Röhm's homosexuality, see Snyder, pp. 297–298.

26. See Glaser, p. 132, and Mosse, who explores such ambivalence throughout his book.

27. See Mosse, pp. 164–165.

28. For the Nazi view of women, see Mosse, pp. 176–180, and Glaser, pp. 178–191.

29. Ernst Christian Helmreich, *The German Churches Under Hitler* (Detroit: Wayne State Univ. Press, 1979), p. 326. See also Mosse, pp. 160–161.

30. Quoted in Glaser, p. 191.

31. See Lifton, p. 149.

32. See Lifton, p. 42.

33. Hitler, *Mein Kampf*, p. 132.

34. Phyllis Grosskurth, *Havelock Ellis: A Biography* (New York: Alfred A. Knopf, 1980), p. 411.

35. Grosskurth, p. 411.

36. Grosskurth, p. 411.

37. See Grosskurth, pp. 414–415.

38. From *Pivot of Civilization* (1922). Quoted by Michael K. Flaherty, "A White Lie," *American Spectator,* August 1992, p. 37, and Elasah Drogin, *Margaret Sanger: Father of Modern Society* (New Hope, KY: Cul Publications, 1986), p. 12. I am indebted to Elizabeth Johnson, one of my students, for her research into Margaret Sanger and her connections to the eugenics movement and to Hitler's programs. Most biographies of Sanger are hagiographical in tone and avoid mention of her racism and her fascist connections. These are fully explored in George Grant, *Grand Illusions: The Legacy of Planned Parenthood* (Brentwood, TN: Wolgemuth and Hyatt, 1988).

39. Quoted in Flaherty, p. 37. See Drogin, p. 33, and J. C. Willke, *Abortion: Questions and Answers* (Cincinnati, OH: Hayes Publishing Co., 1985), p. 290. Grant details Sanger's eugenic theories, pp. 90–94. He also cites her interest in Mussolini's economic theory, p. 42.

40. Quoted in Drogin, p. 17.

41. Debra Braun, *Exposed: Planned Parenthood* (St. Paul, MN: Pro-Life Action Ministries, 1992), p. 5, and Flaherty, p. 37. See Grant, pp. 91–92.

42. Grosskurth, p. 435. Havelock Ellis's works advocating sexual freedom were also banned in post-Röhm Germany.

43. See Lifton, pp. 42–43.

44. Lifton, pp. 25–27.

45. Lifton, p. 48.

46. See Lifton, pp. 46–47. See also Fredric Wertham, *The German Euthanasia*

Program (Cincinnati, OH: Hayes Publishing Co., 1973), pp. 33–34.

47. See Wertham, p. 33.
48. Lifton, p. 49.
49. Lifton, pp. 50–54.
50. From *The Nazi Years: A Documentary History*, ed. Joachim Remak (Prospect Heights, IL: Waveland Press, 1969), pp. 133–134.
51. Wertham, p. 38.
52. Wertham, pp. 30–31.
53. See Lifton, pp. 91–93, who writes of Pastor Braune's document, "Of all recorded expressions of resistance to Nazi medical killing, the Braune memorandum is unique in combining insistent documentation, compassionate identification with victims, concern for healing and healers, focus on the moral integrity of an entire people as well as on the broad ethical principle of the sanctity of life, exposure of the regime's vulnerability to general fear of 'euthanasia' among the military, and passionate personal protest grounded in a spiritual tradition."
54. Lifton, pp. 93–94.
55. Helmreich, p. 338.
56. See Glaser, pp. 55–59.
57. Lifton, p. 154. Of course, "euthanasia" had become a gross misnomer. These people were not given "good" or merciful deaths. Nor were individuals given a say in whether or not they wished to die. Nor was medical killing reserved only for the terminally ill or for those with irreparable brain damage. While the propaganda presented euthanasia in terms of the worst-case scenarios designed to elicit a sympathetic response, the actual practice—once it became morally acceptable on principle—was unspeakably callous, dehumanizing and viciously cruel.

Chapter 7: "The Beautiful Ideas Which Kill"
(pp. 126–144)

1. "Thus Spoke Zarathustra," II.12 in *The Portable Nietzsche*, ed. Walter Kaufmann (New York: Viking, 1968), p. 228.
2. Quoted in Victor Farias, *Heidegger and Nazism*, tr. Paul Burrell (Philadelphia: Temple Univ. Press, 1989), p. 79. From *Die Deutsche Universität im Dritten Reich*, ed. H. Kuhn (Munich, 1966), p. 5.
3. Quoted by Jon Wiener, "Deconstructing de Man," *Nation*, 9 January 1988, p. 23.
4. Alastair Hamilton, *The Appeal of Fascism: A Study of Intellectuals and Fascism, 1919–1945* (New York: Macmillan, 1971), p. xx.
5. Hamilton, p. xv.
6. Zeev Sternhell, "Fascist Ideology," in *Fascism: A Reader's Guide: Analyses, Interpretations, Bibliography* (Berkeley: Univ. of California Press, 1976), p. 322.
7. Modris Eksteins, *Rites of Spring: The Great War and the Birth of the Modern Age* (New York: Houghton Mifflin, 1989), p. 311.

NOTES

8. See Eksteins, pp. 10–54, for a discussion of *The Rites of Spring* and the effect of its original performance.

9. Eksteins, p. 52.

10. See Robert Casillo, *The Genealogy of Demons: Anti-Semitism, Fascism, and the Myths of Ezra Pound* (Evanston, IL: Northwestern Univ. Press, 1988), p. 33.

11. See Hamilton, pp. 280ff.

12. See Wyndham Lewis's book *Hitler* (London: Chatto & Windus, 1931). See also Hamilton, pp. 282-285, and William H. Pritchard, *Wyndham Lewis* (New York: Twayne, 1968), pp. 106–107.

13. See Michael Curtis, *Three Against the Third Republic: Sorel, Barres, and Maurras* (Princeton, NJ: Princeton Univ. Press, 1959), p. 125.

14. See Curtis, p. 130. For the importance of France in the development of fascist ideology, see Zeev Sternhell, *Neither Right nor Left: Fascist Ideology in France,* tr. David Maisel (Berkeley: Univ. of California Press, 1986).

15. See Stephen Spender's Foreword to Hamilton, p. xii. See also Douglas Archibald, *Yeats* (Syracuse, NY: Syracuse Univ. Press, 1983), pp. 146–149, 160.

16. See Hamilton, pp. 277–280.

17. Hamilton, p. 271.

18. See Hamilton, pp. 272–274.

19. See Albert Baugh, *A Literary History of England* (New York: Appleton-Century-Crofts, 1967), p. 1564.

20. See Robert Ferguson, *Enigma: The Life of Knut Hamsun* (New York: Farrar, Straus & Giroux, 1987) and Gaspare Giudice, *Pirandello: A Biography,* tr. Alastair Hamilton (London: Oxford Univ. Press, 1975), pp. 143–165.

21. T. S. Eliot, "The Idea of a Christian Society," in *Christianity and Culture* (New York: Harcourt, Brace & World, 1940), p. 15.

22. See Hamilton, pp. 274–276.

23. See C. David Heymann, *Ezra Pound: The Last Rower* (New York: Viking, 1970), p. 257.

24. "Thus Spoke Zarathustra," I. 15, *Portable Nietzsche,* p. 171.

25. Laurence Lampert, *Nietzsche's Teaching: An Interpretation of "Thus Spoke Zarathustra"* (New Haven, CT: Yale Univ. Press, 1986), p. 245.

26. "Thus Spoke Zarathustra," I. 15, *Portable Nietzsche,* p. 170.

27. Hamilton, xxiix–xiii.

28. See Hamilton, pp. xx–xxi.

29. David H. Hirsch, *The Deconstruction of Literature: Criticism after Auschwitz* (Hanover, NH: Brown Univ. Press, 1991), p. 265.

30. These notes were published in T. J. Reed, *Thomas Mann: The Uses of Tradition* (Oxford: Clarendon Press, 1974), pp. 364–365. Also cited by Hirsch, p. 265.

31. See Sternhell, p. 363, and Robert Soucy, *Fascism in France: The Case of Maurice Barrés* (Berkeley: Univ. of California Press, 1972).

32. Quoted in Sternhell, p. 334. See Andrew Hewitt, "Fascist Modernism, Futurism, and 'Post-modernity,' " in *Fascism, Aesthetics, and Culture,* ed. Richard J. Golsan (Hanover, NH: University Press of New England, 1992), pp. 38–55.

33. Quoted in Sternhell, p. 339.

34. See Jeffrey T. Schnapp, "Epic Demonstrations: Fascist Modernity and the 1932 Exhibition of the Fascist Revolution," in Golsan, pp. 1–37.
35. Schnapp, p. 27.
36. Schnapp, p.22.
37. Quoted in Schnapp, p. 22.
38. See Eksteins, pp. 83–84.
39. Hamilton, p. 135. See Walter A. Strauss, "Gottfried Benn: A Double Life in Uninhabitable Regions," in Golsan, pp. 67–80.
40. See Russell A. Berman, "German Primitivism/Primitive Germany: The Case of Emil Nolde," in Golsan, pp. 55–66.
41. See Hamilton, pp. 152–153. See also George L. Mosse, *Nationalism and Sexuality: Respectability and Abnormal Sexuality in Modern Europe* (New York: Howard Fertig, 1985), p. 162.
42. Robert Hughes, "Culture on the Nazi Pillory," *Time*, 4 March 1991, p. 86. The exhibition was reconstructed in 1991 by Stephanie Barron and the Los Angeles County Museum of Art.
43. Quoted by Hughes, p. 87.
44. Quoted in Mosse, p. 172.
45. National socialism elevated sports to an art form. Hitler promoted the development of "beautiful bodies" through physical education programs in the schools and praised "vanity about a beautiful, well-formed body which everyone can help to build" (*Mein Kampf*, p. 412). Fascist ideology stressed a revolution of the body and of natural sexuality, promoting a cult of physical strength, health, and athleticism. Sports was a test of manliness, an occasion for courage and heroism. With its energizing conflicts, team solidarity, and organized competition, sports was considered the equivalent of war in peacetime. Germany's sponsorship of the 1936 Olympics had special ideological significance for Hitler, with his Aryan athletes taking on the world. The games gave Leni Riefenstahl another occasion to create a cinematic masterpiece, with her documentary film, *Olympia*, which elevated sports to the mythic scale. See Sternhell, pp. 340–341, and Mosse, p. 173.
46. Hughes, p. 87.
47. For the contributions within fascism as related to its art, see Schnapp, pp. 3–4, and Berman, pp. 65–66.

Chapter 8: "The Will to Power"
(pp. 126–144)

1. David H. Hirsch, *The Deconstruction of Literature: Criticism after Auschwitz* (Hanover, NH: Brown Univ. Press, 1991), p. 165.
2. From *Introduction to Metaphysics*. Quoted from Victor Farias, *Heidegger and Nazism*, tr. Paul Burrell (Philadelphia: Temple Univ. Press, 1989), p. 224.
3. The terms *modern* and *postmodern* can also be chronological terms and do not always signal some particular theoretical position. It can be argued that

there is no single postmodern perspective. To speak of a novelist's "postmodern style" may mean something completely different from a critic's "postmodern literary theory." Still, the description of postmodernism I sketch here can serve as a heuristic model that accounts for several strains of contemporary thought, especially those that cluster around the concept of "deconstruction."

4. From his essay "Nietzsche, Genealogy, History," in *Foucault Reader,* ed. Paul Rabinow (New York: Pantheon, 1984), pp. 78–79. See Hirsch, p. 53.

5. See Leonard Jackson, *The Poverty of Structuralism: Literature and Structuralist Theory* (New York: Longman, 1991), pp. 117–121.

6. Hirsch, p. 53.

7. I am referring to my friend Uchey Simon from Nigeria.

8. John M. Ellis, "The Origins of PC," *Chronicle of Higher Education,* 15 January 1992, B1–B2.

9. Ellis, p. B2.

10. Quoted in Farias, p. 229.

11. In *La Critica: Revista di letteratura, storia e filosophia* (Naples), 31 (1933): 69–70. Quoted in Farias, p. 111.

12. See Hirsch, pp. 137–142, et passim. Hirsch has also observed that one could read all of the postmodernist critics without any inkling that the Holocaust had taken place (pp. 69–70).

13. See Hirsch, pp. 18, 75–76, 141–142, 161. Alvin Rosenfeld in *Imagining Hitler* (Bloomington: Indiana Univ. Press, 1985), pp. 105–108, also relates current writers' denial of facticity and history to the suppression of the memory of the Holocaust.

14. Saul Friedlander, "The *Shoah* Between Memory and History," *Jerusalem Quarterly,* 53 (1990), p. 122. Quoted in Hirsch, p. 157.

15. Quoted in Farias, p. 100.

16. See Jon Wiener, "Deconstructing de Man," *Nation,* 9 January 1988, p. 24. See also Jeffrey Mehlman, "Perspectives: on De Man and *Le Soir,*" in *Responses on Paul De Man's Wartime Journalism,* ed. Werner Hamacher, et al. (Lincoln: Univ. of Nebraska Press, 1989), p. 329. J. Hillis Miller, however, denies that Heidegger was a progenitor of deconstruction in "An Open Letter to Professor Jon Wiener," in *Responses,* p. 338.

17. Ward Parks, "Deconstruction: The New Nihilism," *The World & I,* April 1992, p. 548.

18. As an example of how deconstruction is used in literary analysis, *King Lear* can be read in terms of the patriarchal family structure. His daughters are portrayed as villainous because they are rebelling against their overbearing father. Shakespeare is perpetuating a sexist culture, hiding and promoting its oppressive values in beautiful language and a winning story. Such interrogation of an author, like all interrogation, usually ends with the author being convicted of politically incorrect ideas. (On the other hand, authors too are seen as "texts," products of their culture rather than autonomous creators.) But texts deconstruct themselves. Lear's daughters, if the play is read closely enough, have clearly been victimized by their father and are not villains at all. They assert their own power against that of the patriarchal structure and drive their father mad. The patriarchal meaning is countered by a feminist meaning. The play

has a subversive meaning that can be read alongside the official meaning. *King Lear* has been deconstructed.

19. Parks, p. 549.
20. Parks, p. 550.
21. Parks, p. 550.
22. Mehlman, p. 329.
23. See Jeffrey Mehlman, "Maurice Blanchot," in *French Novelists, 1930–1960, Dictionary of Literary Biography* (Detroit: Gale Research, 1988), 72: 77–79. Blanchot wrote for the journals *L'Insurg* and *Combat*. After the war, Mehlman reports, he changed his tone and became a "philosemitic." Mehlman says of him that "he has made of his writing a meditation on the problematic being— or nonbeing—of language, its ultimate incompatibility with self-consciousness, the exhilarating havoc it wreaks on any claim to either objective or subjective identity" (p. 77). See also *Foucault/Blanchot* (New York: Zone Books, 1987), a volume consisting of an essay by Foucault praising Blanchot and an essay by Blanchot praising Foucault.
24. See Hirsch's chapter "Deconstruction and the SS Connection," pp. 143–165.
25. See Wiener, p. 22, and the various essays in *Responses*. For a full account of the De Man scandal, see David Lehman, *Signs of the Times: Deconstruction and the Fall of Paul De Man* (New York: Poseidon Press, 1991).
26. Sternhell, pp. 336–337.
27. See Farias, p. 72.
28. Paul De Man, "The Jews in Contemporary Literature," *Le Soir*, 4 March 1941. Translated by David Lehman and printed in *Signs of the Times*, p. 270.
29. See for example Jacques Derrida, "Like the Sound of the Sea Deep Within a Shell: Paul de Man's War," in *Responses*, pp. 143ff.
30. De Man, "The Jews,", p. 271.
31. See John Brenkman, "Fascist Commitments," in *Responses*, pp. 23ff.
32. Quoted by Stanley Corngold, "On Paul de Man's Collaborationist Writings," *Responses*, p. 83.
33. Paul De Man, *Allegories of Reading* (New Haven, CT: Yale Univ. Press, 1979), p. 296. Discussed by Corngold, p. 83.
34. See the discussions of the passage in Wiener, p. 23 and Mehlman, *Responses*, pp. 329ff.
35. De Man, *Allegories of Reading*, p. 293. "Literary History and Literary Modernity," in *Blindness and Insight* (Minneapolis: Univ. of Minnesota Press, 1983), p. 165. Discussed by Hirsch, pp. 73–74.
36. Hirsch, pp. 73–79.
37. Hirsch, p. 71.
38. For critiques of the deconstructive apologies for De Man, see Parks, pp. 553–555 and Hirsch, pp. 97–103. Compare Derrida's defense of Heidegger in *Of Spirit: Heidegger and the Question* (Chicago: Univ. of Chicago Press, 1989). As Jeffrey Mehlman summarizes his argument, Derrida asserts that Heidegger's Nazism was a humanism (and, conversely, that humanism is a kind of fascism). Derrida's plays on Nazism, fire, exclusion of Jews, and deportation, as Mehlman describes them, amounts to a deconstruction of the Holocaust, which "has,

after all, served as transcendental signified par excellence for two generations" (*Responses*, p. 330).

39. Hirsch, p. 283 n. 12.
40. Susan Handelman, *The Slayers of Moses: The Emergence of Rabbinic Interpretation in Modern Literary Theory* (Albany: State Univ. of New York Press, 1982).
41. Herbert Schneidau, *Sacred Discontent: The Bible and Western Tradition* (Berkeley: Univ. of California Press, 1976).
42. G. Douglas Atkins, *Reading Deconstruction/Deconstructive Reading* (Lexington: Univ. Press of Kentucky, 1983), pp. 41–48.
43. Atkins, pp. 41–42. Atkins, however, quotes Derrida as insisting that his concept of *differance* "is not theological, not even in the most negative order of negative theology" (p. 143).
44. See, for example, Aris Fioretos, "To Read Paul de Man," in *Responses*, pp. 171ff. See also Hirsch, p. 95, pp. 113–115.
45. "Thus Spoke Zarathustra," II.12 in *The Portable Nietzsche*, ed. Walter Kaufmann (New York: Viking, 1968), p. 228.
46. Ernst Nolte, *Three Faces of Fascism: Action Française, Italian Fascism, National Socialism*, trans. Leila Vennewitz (New York: Holt, Rinehart & Winston, 1965), p. 429.
47. Parks, p. 554.
48. Parks, p. 554.
49. Hirsch, p. 87.
50. Goethe, "Faust (Part One)," tr. Louis MacNeice in *Great Writings of Goethe*, ed. Stephen Spender (New York: New American Library, 1958), p.70.
51. See Harry Redner, *In the Beginning was the Deed: Reflections on the Passage of Faust* (Berkeley: Univ. of California Press, 1982), pp.41–77. Redner's entire book is an exploration of this passage and the Faust legend as they relate to modern and postmodern thought. Redner shows how language itself has been progressively interpreted as mind, power, and deed. He also discusses the passage as it relates to Nietzsche, Heidegger, and Foucault. Redner relates the apotheosis of the deed to the interplay between progress and nihilism. He likewise raises the specter of Auschwitz as one of the consequences of the modern Faustian bargain.
52. Goethe, "Faust," pp.92–93.
53. Germany has always seen itself reflected in Goethe's *Faust*. See Jane K. Brown, *Goethe's Faust: The German Tragedy* (Ithaca, NY: Cornell Univ. Press, 1986), pp. 10–11. A number of German authors and filmmakers have related the Faust legend to Germany's experiment with fascism. The most profound exploration of this theme is Thomas Mann's novel *Doctor Faustus*. See Redner, p. 41, pp.241ff.

Chapter 9: "The People's Culture"
(pp. 145–160)

1. Martin Heidegger's wife, from one of her pro-Nazi articles. Quoted in Victor Farias, *Heidegger and Nazism*, tr. Paul Burrell (Philadelphia: Temple Univ. Press, 1989), p. 229.

2. Marshall McLuhan, *The Medium is the Massage* (New York: Random House, 1967), p. 63.

3. Neil Postman, *Teaching as a Conserving Activity* (New York: Delacorte Press, 1979), pp. 47–70.

4. Postman, *Teaching as a Conserving Activity*, p. 57.

5. Postman, *Teaching as a Conserving Activity*, p. 77.

6. Neil Postman, *Amusing Ourselves to Death: Public Discourse in the Age of Show Business* (New York: Viking, 1985).

7. Adolf Hitler, *Mein Kampf*, tr. Ralph Manheim (Boston: Houghton Mifflin, 1943), p. 470. The italics are Hitler's.

8. From *Introduction to Metaphysics*. Quoted from Farias, p. 224.

9. Jon Wiener, "Deconstructing de Man," *Nation*, 9 January 1988, p. 23.

10. Farias, p. 116.

11. Louis Snyder, *Encyclopedia of the Third Reich* (New York: McGraw-Hill, 1976), pp. 93–94.

12. See Postman, *Amusing Ourselves to Death*, pp. 30–43, 125–141.

13. From *Niederelbisches Tageblatt*. September 12, 1936, in Hans-Jochen Gamm, *Der braune Kult* (Hamburg, 1962), pp. 55–56. In *The Nazi Years: A Documentary History*, ed. Joachim Remak (Prospect Heights, IL: Waveland Press, 1990), pp. 79–80.

14. Hitler, p. 479.

15. Hitler, p. 469. The italics are his.

16. See, for example, Kenneth Myers, *All God's Children and Blue Suede Shoes: Christians and Popular Culture* (Westchester, IL: Crossway Books, 1989).

17. See Marshall McLuhan, *Understanding Media: The Extensions of Man* (New York: New American Library, 1964), pp. 30–31, 38, 58–59.

18. See John M. Ellis, "The Origins of PC," *Chronicle of Higher Education*, 15 January 1992, p. B2.

19. Franz Kerber, "People, Culture, and Town," quoted in Farias, p. 242.

20. See Hermann Glaser, *The Cultural Roots of National Socialism*, trans. Ernest A. Menze (Austin: Univ. of Texas Press, 1978), pp. 86–93. See also Modris Eksteins, *Rites of Spring: The Great War and the Birth of the Modern Age* (New York: Houghton Mifflin, 1989), p. 304.

21. Quoted by Zeev Sternhell, "Fascist Ideology," in *Fascism: A Reader's Guide,* ed. Walter Laqueur (Berkeley: Univ. of California Press, 1976), p. 334.

22. Quoted by Sternhell, p. 320.

23. See Bill Buford, "The Lads of the National Front," *New York Times Magazine*, 26 April 1992, pp. 32ff. For a report on American Skinheads and their ties to white supremacy movements and to punk rock, see Ellen Uzelac, "Skinheads Trained for Hate Role," *Milwaukee Journal*, [Syndicated by *Baltimore Sun*], 8 January 1989, p. J1.

24. Quoted in David H. Hirsch, *The Deconstruction of Literature: Criticism after Auschwitz* (Hanover, NH: Brown Univ. Press, 1991), pp. 124–125.

25. Quoted in Max Weinreich, *Hitler's Professors: The Part of Scholarship in Germany's Crimes against the Jewish People* (New York: Yiddish Scientific Institute, 1946), p. 159.

26. Hannah Arendt, *The Origins of Totalitarianism* (New York: Harcourt, Brace & World, 1951), pp. 341–364.

27. Quoted in Farias, p. 230.

28. See Uzelac, p. J2.

29. A point made to me by the Estonian poet and activist Hasso Krull.

30. See Buford, p. 42.

31. Paul De Man, "The Jews in Contemporary Literature," *Le Soir*, 4 March 1941. Translated by David Lehman. Printed in David Lehman, *Signs of the Times: Deconstruction and the Fall of Paul De Man* (New York: Poseidon Press, 1991), pp. 269–270.

32. George Steiner, *In Bluebeard's Castle: Some Notes Towards the Redefinition of Culture* (New Haven, CT: Yale Univ. Press, 1971), p. 41.

Index

Gene Edward Veith, Jr., is Associate Professor of English and Dean of the College of Arts and Sciences at Concordia University Wisconsin, Mequon, WI.

Born in Alva, OK, Veith holds a B.A. in Letters with Distinction from the University of Oklahoma (1972), a M.A. in English from the University of Kansas (1975), and a Ph.D. in English from the University of Kansas (1979).

He is the author of *Loving God with All Your Mind; Reading Between the Lines; State of the Arts: From Bezalel to Mapplethorpe* (all by Crossway Books); *The Gift of Art: The Place of the Arts in Scripture* (InterVarsity Press); *Reformation Spirituality: The Religion of George Herbert* (Bucknell U. Press); and numerous articles and book reviews.

Dr. Veith and his wife, Jackquelyn, have three children, Paul, Joanna, and Mary.